Transforming Museum Management

Museums must change to illuminate the histories, cultures, and social issues that matter to their local population. Based on a unique longitudinal ethnographic study, *Transforming Museum Management* illustrates how a traditional art museum attempted to transform into a more inclusive and community-based institution.

Using open systems theory and the Buddhist concept of mutual causality, it examines the museum's internal management structure and culture, programs and exhibitions, and mental models of museum workers. In providing both theoretical and practical foundations to transform management structures, this accessible volume will benefit stakeholders by proposing a new culture and structure to arts institutions, to change practice to be more relevant, diverse, and inclusive.

This book will be an invaluable resource for researchers and advanced students of museum studies, cultural management, arts administration, nonprofit management, and organizational studies.

Yuha Jung, PhD, is an associate professor of Arts Administration at the University of Kentucky in the United States. She is also an associate editor for the journal *Museum Management and Curatorship* and a board member of the Association of Arts Administration Educators.

Routledge Research in the Creative and Cultural Industries
Series Editor: Ruth Rentschler

This series brings together book-length original research in cultural and creative industries from a range of perspectives. Charting developments in contemporary cultural and creative industries thinking around the world, the series aims to shape the research agenda to reflect the expanding significance of the creative sector in a globalised world.

Digital Transformation in the Cultural and Creative Industries
Production, Consumption and Entrepreneurship in the Digital and Sharing Economy
Edited by Marta Massi, Marilena Vecco and Yi Lin

Researching Arts Markets
Past, Present and Tools for the Future
Edited by Elisabetta Lazzaro, Nathalie Moureau and Adriana Turpin

Strategic Cultural Centre Management
Tomas Järvinen

The Music Export Business
Born Global
Stephen Chen, Shane Homan and Tracy Redhead

Cultural Management and Policy in Latin America
Edited by Raphaela Henze and Federico Escribal

Transforming Museum Management
Evidence-Based Change through Open Systems Theory
Yuha Jung

For more information about this series, please visit: www.routledge.com/Routledge-Research-in-the-Creative-and-Cultural-Industries/book-series/RRCCI

"Museums and galleries cannot exist in isolation from their diverse communities, and it is painful to note that far too many persist in doing so. Yuha Jung is acutely aware of this and her book provides a framework for learning, disorganizing, and reorganizing. Building on her earlier work on open systems, and now adding the Buddhist concept of interdependence, she charts a course for all museums wishing to provide meaning and value in these troubled times."

— *Robert R. Janes, Founder and Co-Chair of Coalition of Museums for Climate Justice*

Transforming Museum Management
Evidence-Based Change through Open Systems Theory

Yuha Jung

LONDON AND NEW YORK

First published 2022
by Routledge
2 Park Square, Milton Park, Abingdon, Oxon OX14 4RN

and by Routledge
605 Third Avenue, New York, NY 10158

Routledge is an imprint of the Taylor & Francis Group, an informa business

© 2022 Yuha Jung

The right of Yuha Jung to be identified as author of this work has been asserted by her in accordance with sections 77 and 78 of the Copyright, Designs and Patents Act 1988.

All rights reserved. No part of this book may be reprinted or reproduced or utilised in any form or by any electronic, mechanical, or other means, now known or hereafter invented, including photocopying and recording, or in any information storage or retrieval system, without permission in writing from the publishers.

Trademark notice: Product or corporate names may be trademarks or registered trademarks, and are used only for identification and explanation without intent to infringe.

British Library Cataloguing-in-Publication Data
A catalogue record for this book is available from the British Library

Library of Congress Cataloging-in-Publication Data
Names: Jung, Yuha, author.
Title: Transforming museum management : evidence-based change through open systems theory / Yuha Jung.
Description: London ; New York, NY : Routledge/Taylor & Francis Group, 2021. |
Series: Routledge research in the creative and cultural industries | Includes bibliographical references and index. |
Identifiers: LCCN 2021001927 (print) | LCCN 2021001928 (ebook) | ISBN 9780367136031 (hardcover) | ISBN 9780367136048 (ebook)
Subjects: LCSH: Museums—Management. | System theory. | Organizational change.
Classification: LCC AM121 .J68 2021 (print) | LCC AM121 (ebook) | DDC 069/.068—dc23
LC record available at https://lccn.loc.gov/2021001927
LC ebook record available at https://lccn.loc.gov/2021001928

ISBN: 978-0-367-13603-1 (hbk)
ISBN: 978-1-032-03009-8 (pbk)
ISBN: 978-0-367-13604-8 (ebk)

Typeset in Times New Roman
by codeMantra

Contents

List of figures ix
Preface xi
Acknowledgments xvii

1 Introduction to research and methodology 1

2 Open systems theory and mutual causality 17

3 Entangled realities between the museum and its community 31

4 Museum throughputs and mental models 49

5 Outputs and outcomes of museum change 69

6 Toward a deep learning museum and paradigm shift 88

*Appendix A: list of key participants' pseudonyms
and their affiliations* 109
Index 111

Figures

2.1	Open Systems Organization and Its Feedback Functions	24
3.1	River Cities Community Joined and Divided by the Central River	31
4.1	Avery Art Museum Organizational Chart	50
5.1	Comparison of Community and Avery Visitor Demographics	80
6.1	Open Systems Museum and Its Feedback Functions	89

Preface

This research journey started in 2011, almost ten years ago from the time of writing. I visited the Avery Art Museum (a pseudonym), in the summer of 2011 for the first time for my dissertation research, which I completed at the end of 2012. Since then, I returned to the same museum two more times in 2015 and 2019, recording the progress and changes over time. While I had a general idea and theoretical framework for this book, I completed the final analysis of the study and shaped the detailed structure of the book in the final eight months of writing from May to December 2020. The entire process of collecting data, analyzing the data, and writing took about nine years from the time I collected the initial data for my dissertation, not knowing it would become a much larger study and eventually a book. This book shares some ideas from my dissertation but has evolved to become much different.

The theoretical frameworks I use in this book are open systems theory and mutual causality of Buddhism. These two are parallel ideas found in both Eastern and Western philosophies. Systems theory resonated with me ever since I first encountered it during my doctoral studies at Penn State. How people, things, organizations, and societies coexist in a nested structure interdependent of and with each other made a lot of sense. The Buddhist teachings of mutual causality also emphasize the inseparable realities of body and mind, actors and organizations, and organizations and their larger environment mutually affecting each other. Growing up in a family that believed deeply in Buddhism, it was only a matter of time before I turned to the familiar. Additionally, I wanted to bring a perspective that is not just Western theory or philosophy that can be overrepresented in the academic world.

With the changing external environment, museums must change to meet the new challenges and new needs of their community. Museums can change, but they need a systemic and paradigm shifting model for long-lasting and meaningful transformation. They must move past their history of elitism and white privilege, and start anew with a renewed mindset, networked management system, collaborative culture, and genuine attention to broader audiences who may not have ever seen the inside of a museum. This book is an attempt to suggest ways for museums to transform to be relevant and inclusive places. While the theories I use in this book may seem complex, the core idea is simple. We can make museum open systems networked and somewhat vulnerable to new ideas in order to help them become inclusive in creating exhibitions and programs rather than generating content based on assumptions and guesswork.

In this book, I talk about negative and positive feedback functions based on open systems theory and the concept of mutual causality; a negative feedback mechanism stabilizes an organization by maintaining the status quo while a positive feedback function reorganizes and renews the organization to meet the changing needs of the external environment making it relevant to external pressures. An open organization needs both negative and positive feedback functions to sustain itself, but without consistently triggering a positive feedback function, it can become an obsolete organization, for example, that is only relevant to a small group of people.

I gave a pseudonym, the Avery Art Museum, to the subject museum and other participants as well as names of cites, regions, and states to protect the identity of the museum and participants, following the rules and regulations of the Institutional Review Board. Confidentiality also provides me the academic freedom to discuss what I observed, heard, recorded, and synthesized without being concerned about people finding out the real identity of actors. Therefore, I do not reveal the state where the museum is located. Rather, I call it the North State. River Cities is used instead of the metropolitan area name where the museum is located. Watertown replaces the actual city name the Avery is part of. To organize the participants in relation to their pseudonyms and affiliations, I created the Appendix A: List of Key Participants' Pseudonyms and Their Affiliations. This list does not include all 200 interview participants. Rather, it lists participants whom I quoted more than once. Additionally, citation information or any specific data containing elements that could identify participants, the subject museum, or its location has been withheld or modified.

Outline of this book

This book has six chapters. Chapter 1 introduces the book and research, and Chapter 2 discusses the theories in depth. Chapters 3–5 are the main analyses of the study sharing recorded changes or stagnation of the museum in many different areas following the mutually affecting feedback mechanism of an open system. Chapter 3 discusses how the museum as an open system is interconnected with and disconnected from its larger environment. Chapter 4 is about the throughputs (e.g., management structure and workplace culture) of the museum open system and museum actors' mental models that transform inputs (e.g., information and resources) to outputs (e.g., exhibitions and programs). Chapter 5 discusses outputs of the museum open system and effects of the outputs. Chapter 6 concludes the book by

Preface xiii

presenting an open systems change model or theory that fully utilizes a positive feedback function. Below, I include more detailed chapter summaries.

Chapter 1 starts with a brief overview of the theories of open systems and mutual casualty followed by research questions that investigate the interconnections and changes between the museum and its community over time. It also discusses the significance of research that is relevant to the current state of the field, develops a field-specific theory, describes the book's usefulness to both scholars and practitioners, and advances methodology to study museums. Additionally, it introduces the subject museum and the rationale for choosing it as my research subject. Lastly, this chapter will discuss the methodology in full including the general philosophical and methodological approaches of symbolic, holistic, and longitudinal ethnography followed by a detailed research design on data collection, analysis, and interpretation, and limitations of the methods and methodology.

Chapter 2 lays out the theoretical foundation for the study to examine the museum and its community and why this theory is appropriate to study museums. Open systems theory and the Buddhist teaching of mutual causality define organizations as existing in a layered and networked structure that are mutually affecting and dependent on their external environment. Museums as open systems exist within their larger environment, and their parts are interdependent and interconnected. They are flexible and adaptable, exist in holarchy, and stabilize or renew through negative or positive feedback functions of mutual causality. A negative feedback mechanism stabilizes an organization by reducing deviations between internal practice and external pressure, while a positive feedback function renews the organization by encouraging the deviations, disorganization, and reorganization. Considering new and diverse inputs can help trigger a positive feedback function, which helps transform mental models of museum actors—the most ingrained assumptions of the organization—and throughputs of structure and culture within an organization. This chapter also emphasizes the concept of systems intelligence, which is a way of thinking about actors as part of the larger system and in relation to other parts and actors within the system. Systems intelligence can help transform actors' mental models and their actions, creating an environment where actors can learn and grow together in solving issues using a system-wide solution. Applying this model can lead to a field-wide paradigm shift.

Chapter 3 demonstrates how the museum is part of its community by applying open systems theory. It specifically discusses the interconnected and disconnected realities between the museum and its community. To explain the interconnections, the chapter examines the developmental history of the museum in relation to its city, the museum's role in revitalizing the economy, the history of museum funding based on a public and private partnership, the museum's vital role as an educational place, and its collaboration with other community arts and cultural organizations. The disconnected realities between the museum and the community were shown by the community's elitist perception about the museum, the community's attitude toward the intimidating look of the museum building, the community's fear of art and lack of cultural capital, and discrepancies between the demographics of the community and those of the staff, board, and core visitors. While disconnections and discrepancies may present challenges, they also present a perfect condition for the museum to trigger a positive feedback function that will urge the museum to disorganize and reorganize to gather more input to match the needs of the wider community, not just those of a narrow group.

Chapter 4 discusses the management structure and workplace culture of the museum's complex internal system. The structure and culture of the museum represent throughputs where the museum transforms inputs (e.g., resources and information) into outputs (e.g., programs and exhibitions). The structure represents board structure, leadership, and departmental organization. The cultural throughput represents the workplace culture, communications, and collaboration among staff and departments. The structure and culture are based on the internal actors' mental models or assumptions that have evolved over time. Although there had been some positive disruptions—new leadership and more collaboration among departments—to the museum's throughputs, the internal system of the museum stagnated following the status quo ways of thinking and doing things. It needed a shift in mental models to challenge the old ways of practice. By embracing systems intelligence and system leadership collectively, which can help see how their actions influence others and the overall goals of the museum, the museum can trigger a positive feedback function toward transformative change.

Chapter 5 is about outputs of the museum open system. Primary outputs of a museum are exhibitions and programs. Outcomes are the consequences and effects of the outputs. The throughputs of structure and culture and the actors' mental models necessarily influence the museum's core service areas of exhibitions and programs. While the throughputs and actors of the museum generated more diverse and innovative outputs and made it possible to establish a new network-based funding model, affecting future outputs of the museum, the consequence of the outputs showed that the museum was not fully inclusive. The museum's core visitors represented a small group of homogeneous and privileged population. To close the gap between the core museum users and the community demographics, the museum needs to reorganize its throughputs and challenge its mental models to gain new and collective intelligence or become a learning museum that grows and renews itself to be relevant and inclusive.

Chapter 6 concludes the book by presenting a model of an open systems museum and its feedback functions. This model describes how a museum can become a learning organization using specific examples and suggestions. Examples of complete loops of both negative and positive feedback functions from the Avery demonstrate how the mechanism works in a real-life setting. An example of a positive feedback function is the museum's successful transformation from a traditional funding model into a networked funding structure relying on multiple levels and sources of funding. An example of a negative feedback function is the museum's stagnation in organizational communication and collaboration and diversity in its visitorship. The museum lacked intentional cultural and structural changes that required a shift in mental models. By actively seeking new inputs from its wider community, the museum can trigger a positive feedback function and maintain dynamic equilibrium, an inter-state of a system that is always prepared to make changes. To trigger a positive feedback loop and maintain dynamic equilibrium, this final chapter presents a museum change model where museums can pay attention to several leverage points at each level of the feedback loop. Additionally, this model addresses how the external environment of museums (through professional association practice and policy-level changes) can generate pressure points in creating conditions for museum practice to change. Effective adoption and practice of positive feedback functions can transform museums to become deep learning museums where actors truly understand the mutual interconnection between their work and larger community, and continuously learn and grow to be relevant and inclusive. When applied widely to many museums and accepted as a legitimate way of practice, this model has a potential to ultimately shift a field-wide practice paradigm to be inclusive and relevant.

Acknowledgments

I thank my parents for their unconditional love and support. They always let me try and fail, so I could find my own path, even though that meant living far away from each other on the opposite side of the hemisphere. I thank Sarah Grainger, my long-time friend and professional editor, for being a sound critique and an effective editor for more than ten years. I appreciate Sarah's honesty and insights which helped keep me in check for the entire process of writing this book. I appreciate my dean, chair, and colleagues for letting me keep my sabbatical in the fall of 2020 to complete the book, even though it was a difficult time for the entire university and put extra constraints on my department and colleagues. I thank the Avery Art Museum, the subject of this book, for allowing me to study it, and I thank the people who worked there for letting me in their space and ask questions. I thank Terry Clague, Senior Publisher, and Adam Woods, editorial assistant, of Routledge for making this book possible and keeping me on track while being flexible. Lastly, I thank my Nino for encouraging me along the way every time I hit a block and was tired of writing.

1 Introduction to research and methodology

Concepts of open systems and mutual causality

Open systems theory postulates that organizations cannot exist in isolation from their communities. While the extent of their influence on each other can vary, the interconnection among different parts within an organization, among organizations, and with the larger community affects organizational outputs, survival, long-term goals, and renewal. The actors and parts within an organization always influence each other and those of external elements in a mutual fashion. This differs from unidirectional influence, as in a linear cause-and-effect relationship, where one can identify the cause, its origin, and its exact effect. Rather, within open systems theory, the cause and effect of many different variables are difficult to pinpoint as they affect each other in multi-directional and interdependent ways. This concept of mutual casualty is at the heart of open systems theory as well as that of early Buddhist teachings, making it an ancient concept that emerged from both Western and Eastern philosophies.

Looking at a museum as an open social system, its elements are interdependent and also part of the larger environment. This study examines the whole museum as part of its community rather than examining either the museum separately from its community or one section of the museum, such as its educational or curatorial functions. Therefore, while the Avery Art Museum is the subject of the research, it is not the sole focus because it cannot be understood in isolation from its subsystems (e.g., actors, departments, and culture) or suprasystems (e.g., economic and political systems of the community). Based on three ethnographic moments of 2011, 2015, and 2019, I examined how change happened and did not happen at the Avery. This long-term study is used as an interpretive example to demonstrate how open systems theory and its concept of mutual casualty form a theory of change that is applicable to real-life settings. More in-depth discussion of open systems theory and mutual causality is the topic of Chapter 2.

Research questions

The book aims to provide a theory of change or paradigm shifting model that could lead to sustainable and transformational changes of this museum and many other museums to become more diverse, inclusive, and relevant and become fully integrated parts of their community. More specifically, it examines: (1) how the art museum is connected to or disconnected from its community; (2) how internal workings of the museum, such as management structure and workplace culture, change or stagnate over time; (3) how internal workings and external factors of the museum transformed its primary service provisions and practices; and (4) what are some of the ways the museum can transform to be more relevant and inclusive for the changing demographics, needs, and demands of the larger environment.

To explore these inquiries, I describe a detailed and longitudinal account of an art museum practice from multiple perspectives, including what has changed, what has not changed, and what affected those results. I also theorize an effective change process in a way that can be used by others, presenting a paradigm shifting model in Chapter 6. While this book is not attempting to generalize and provide a model for all museums, it can show how one museum struggled to change by providing various in-depth understandings of the museum internally and externally, and by showing its complicated processes, multiple actors involved, and environmental factors considered. Its detailed and long-term accounts of change descriptions can be helpful for many museums to reflect on their own practices and see how the change model can be applied to their situation. Chapters 3–5 include very detailed and descriptive accounts of the museum's connection and disconnection to its community; its internal workings, culture, and structural changes over time; and how these elements have affected the museum practices. Chapter 6 will tie these chapters together in creating a museum-specific model of change based on open systems theory and mutual causality of feedback functions.

Significance of the research

The research is significant in several ways: (1) it emphasizes the importance of diversity and inclusion in museums that have been an ongoing and stubborn issue of the sector for decades; (2) it attempts to develop a theory specific for museum governance and administration; (3) it is both theoretical and practical and therefore can be useful to multiple stakeholders; and, lastly, (4) it contributes to the development of research methodology in social anthropology and museum studies.

First, it speaks directly to the pressing issue of museums that are not diverse in their collections, people, and programming and not inclusive in creating their services and hiring their people. This study emphasizes the importance of diversity and inclusion in a broad sense because open systems theory and the concept of mutual causality value the diversity of inputs (e.g., information, data, and resources), inclusive processes of throughputs (e.g., inclusive culture and valuing of different ideas), and diverse outputs (e.g., diverse programs serving different groups of people). In this book, diversity is defined as ways that people are different within organizations (AAM 2018) as well as different ideas they bring in. Additionally, I use it narrowly referring to race, ethnicity, gender, sexual orientation, socioeconomic status, educational levels, and more. While all of these different groups are important, I tend to emphasize race and socioeconomic status in this research as they are the most relevant issues related to the subject museum and for most art museums in the United States and perhaps in different countries. Inclusion is defined as intentional efforts for diverse individuals and their ideas to be reflected in every level and decision-making process of an organization (AAM 2018). Without the intentional practice of including various voices and groups in decision-making processes, diversity of people and differences of ideas will not be properly utilized. This emphasis on diversity and inclusion found in the theory of open systems and mutual casualty resonates with the pressing issue of the current environment of the museum world that it is not inclusive nor relevant enough for changing demographics and socioeconomic and political climates (Anderson 2020; Boucher 2020). I address ways museums can be more inclusive and diverse regarding internal decision-making, museum services, funding sources, staff composition, and audience development.

Second, I explain how museums' outputs (e.g., exhibitions, programs, and events) are related to their internal structure, workplace culture, and assumptions of the actors, proposing a holistic way to operate museums in relation to many elements both inside and outside the museum. This type of organic, holistic, and more human resources-oriented methods of governing and managing museums have gained attention over the past decades (Bergeron and Tuttle 2013; Lord and Blankenberg 2015; Moore 1994), but there are few in-depth studies conducted illustrating this type of practice in real-life examples with empirical data. Many cultural organizations still follow the mechanical management system that is borrowed from outdated for-profit business practices (Falk and Sheppard 2006; Janes and Sandell 2019; Moore 1994). This book proposes a different theory of museum management, factoring in the unique context of museums as cultural and educational places that are philosophically and structurally different from for-profit businesses. As the book is concerned with holistic governing and management systems through incorporating open systems theory and mutual casualty feedback functions, it will touch on many different areas of operation, including leadership, communication, marketing, and funding.

Third, this book would ideally provide both theoretical and practical foundations for art museums to transform in function and better serve the diverse publics through improved practices. Therefore, this book can benefit multiple stakeholders—scholars, practitioners, and graduate students—by providing an alternative framework to examine museums, proposing a new structure to manage museums, and influencing museums' practices to focus more on the needs and interests of diverse groups of people. Beyond its contribution to scholarship, the study aims to encourage art museum professionals to understand the connections between their museums and the communities that they serve. This research, although not universally generalizable, can benefit museum directors, trustees, educators, curators, and other museum professionals. While the subject museum is an art museum, the result may be useful for other arts and cultural workers because there are many shared characteristics and challenges among nonprofit cultural and educational organizations.

Lastly, this book contributes to research methodologies for investigating organizations. In organizational anthropology, there has been a relatively recent gap that has formed between organizational behavior and anthropology (Bate 1997). While it is common to think of organizational behavior as a sub-discipline of business administration, it originated from social anthropology (Whyte 1969). My research addresses the organizational behavior and workplace culture of a museum as a social anthropological study using longitudinal ethnography, an underused methodology in examining organizations (Bate 1997). Longitudinal ethnography has rarely, if ever, been used in studying museums. Therefore, this book not only fills the gap between organizational behavior and anthropology but also renews ethnography as a useful methodology to examine organizations that can be used by scholars of other cultural management and museum studies.

Description of the subject museum and its community

The subject museum is the Avery Art Museum, located in Watertown, which is the largest city in the River Cities area. River Cities is a medium-sized metropolitan area composed of several cities and towns in the Midwestern United States. River Cities has an estimated population of less than a half million (all identifiable information has been modified to preserve anonymity and confidentiality). Traditionally, farming and manufacturing have been the dominant industries of the area, although by the early 2000s, its economy has expanded to include healthcare, education, and information technology. About 20% of the population holds a bachelor's degree or higher. Study participants described the River Cities as largely a blue-collar community.

The Avery Family Foundation, established by an affluent family, donated about a third of a $45 million construction project. The museum relocated downtown in a new building with a new name in the mid-2000s. While these changes gave the museum a different identity, its precursor was the municipal art gallery established in the 1920s. This shows a long history and existence of this museum in its community. Prior to its move to downtown, the city of Watertown provided the museum's funding and hired its employees. When the museum became the Avery in its new location with its new identity, the city agreed to provide about 30% of the museum's annual operating budget for a set period of time.

The Avery is a medium-sized art museum. While the size of the building is quite large, approximately 120,000 square feet, the museum employed only 17 full-time staff members and 4 part-time staff members along with a number of volunteers, docents, and interns in 2019. The staff size virtually stayed the same having 16 full-time staff members and 5 part-time staff members in 2011. The annual operating budget was about $2 million in 2011 and increased to be more than $3 million by 2019. More than a half of the museum space is dedicated to education, including studios, library, children's gallery, auditorium, store, and lobby. The museum mostly collected American, European, Caribbean, Central American, and Asian arts. After the move, its targeted areas expanded from serving only Watertown to include the greater River Cities area. With its new modern building downtown opened to the public in the middle of the 2000s, the museum had been operating as a "new" organization for several years when I first visited it.

Rationale for selecting the Avery as the research site

There were three reasons for choosing the Avery. First, with the Avery, I could tell a story of a relatively smaller art museum that has a homogeneous rather than diverse population. Many published studies in the museum field highlight best practices of large and better-known museums in highly populated metropolitan areas. My experiences in professional and academic conferences confirm that museum research tends to focus on museums that are larger and more successful with substantial financial and human resources. Much less is known about how small- to medium-sized museums with limited funding and human resources are relevant and active in their communities. According to a benchmarking report by the Association of Art Museum Directors (2018), 40% of museums surveyed reported having less than $5 million for its operating budget. The Avery had less than $4 million operating budget in 2019 so it belongs in this smallest budget size category in this report. An extreme example of a large museum is the Metropolitan Museum of Art, which spent over $492 million in the 2018 fiscal year (2019). Many smaller museums are often located in more homogenous areas, facing characteristic challenges in connecting with their communities and providing meaningful experiences for them, often requiring a distinctive type of museum practice that is drastically different from running a large, better funded, and tourist-attracting museum. I chose the Avery as a chance to understand the challenges and practices of smaller museums in the field of museum studies.

Second, I selected the Avery because I had never visited the museum or its geographical region prior to data collection. I thought I would see such a museum and community with fresher eyes than examining a museum that

I was familiar with. Since I had never visited the museum or its region prior to commencement of the first study in 2011, I could be more impartial in understanding the Avery and therefore could include as many diverse views as possible from participants, rather than projecting my own view. I became much more familiar with the museum and its region as I visited the area two more times, although I felt out of place in most places in River Cities even during my most recent visit in 2019 due to my racial, ethnic, and cultural backgrounds. Nevertheless, I had assumptions and biases about the Midwest before I started collecting data, which I explain in the "Limitations of the methods and methodology" section below.

This last point may be the most important one, making this work possible. As one can imagine, a researcher cannot simply show up at a museum she wants to study and it welcomes her into its internal workings. It is not a comfortable thing for museums to be open to a stranger. I was lucky to meet a museum scholar and professional who was affiliated with the Avery at a museum conference. I was about to embark on my doctoral research and was looking for a participant museum. She suggested that I come to the Avery because my work could be beneficial for the museum. She acted as a bridge connecting me to the museum. I do not think the museum would have been welcome to have me there initially without this connection. When I arrived at the museum the first time, I found that its staff members were welcoming and showed an interest in my exploration. I am grateful for their willingness to open up to a stranger.

Methodology: longitudinal ethnography

The study's overarching methodology is ethnography mostly based on interviews and participant observations. I stayed in River Cities for two months each in the summer of 2011 and 2015 and three weeks in 2019. In telling a deep story of organizational changes of a museum in relation to its community over time, the three ethnographic moments are woven together into one monograph conceptualizing change processes.

Symbolic perspective of the methodology

The overarching methodological philosophy is symbolic perspective, which values multiple meanings of interpretations and focuses on interpretive processes to understand and interpret organizations and their practices and processes (Hatch 2018). Symbolic theorists recognize multiple understandings and interpretations of reality, valuing individual interpretations of various parts of organizations and their environment. Based on these beliefs, symbolic researchers allow themselves to be immersed in the context and embrace interpretivist epistemology, which assumes that "knowledge can only be created and understood from within the contexts" (Hatch 2018, 15). Because symbolists believe that subjective social constructs of organizations, their culture, and environment can be more effectively understood by the interpretive processes, they use qualitative methodologies, immersing themselves in the everyday workings of an organization under study. Ethnography is a good example of a qualitative method that symbolic organization researchers use to identify the informal structure and unsaid rules and cultures of organizations by observing people's behaviors and the meanings behind them. Ethnography rejects pure naturalism that presupposes that cultures and relationships can be understood as they are, without the influence of researchers (Hammersley and Atkinson 2007). Rather, ethnographers tend to view society as constructed, and they acknowledge that researchers necessarily influence the descriptions and conclusions of ethnographic studies by their perspectives (Hammersley and Atkinson, 2007).

I follow symbolic theorist views of knowledge and understanding of the world. Museum actors' thoughts and feelings are important in understanding the inner workings of the museum and their practices in relation to the larger community. That is why I stayed in the region as long as I could each time I visited and went into the museum almost every day to "feel" and "experience" the organization within its environmental context.

Holistic and longitudinal ethnography

Based on the symbolic view, ethnography is suitable for illuminating the complex interactions of the museum and its community. Ethnographic methods are considered an ideal tool for understanding the culture and systems of an organization in relation to its surroundings (Geertz 1973). Ethnographic research was originally developed by anthropologists as a way to understand specific cultures and groups within their social, cultural, economic, and spatial contexts. In its original manifestation, it was often associated with the concept of *otherness* to comprehend people and culture other than the mainstream Western culture (Hammersley and Atkinson 2007; Merriam 2002; Tedlock 2000; Wolcott 2008). This relatively narrow view of ethnography has expanded to becoming a well-acknowledged research methodology in various fields such as cultural studies, education, industrial engineering, and health services (Hammersley and Atkinson 2007; Tedlock 2000; Tørring et al. 2019).

This work, while utilizing traditional ethnographic methods, provides a new perspective on the operation of small- to medium-sized museums since this type of ethnographic study about a museum in its larger surroundings is rarely used, especially adopting a longer-term perspective. One ethnographic work that inspired my research design is *Ain't No Makin' It: Aspirations and Attainment in a Low-Income Neighborhood* by MacLeod (2009). This research investigated a social phenomenon through looking at the surrounding elements and contexts using ethnography rather than just focusing on the subject under investigation. For example, his work investigates how social reproduction (e.g., inequity reproduced from one generation to another) is actualized in two distinctive brotherhood groups in a socioeconomically depressed area of the United States. He investigated the boys' personal, educational, social, and economic lives in order to understand their culture holistically (MacLeod, 2009). In other words, rather than just observing and interviewing two groups of boys and looking at narrow aspects such as race and poverty, he investigated their surroundings and personal life, including family situations, school life, and their relationships to other peers and teachers. This research was conducted over a long period of time. After the initial study, MacLeod revisited his participants two more times, showing how the participants' lives had changed into their adulthood. His approach to the subject was multi-faceted and holistic, including the surrounding networks of the two groups.

I adopted MacLeod's research approach, which is apparent in my research design. My work is based on the premise that we can best understand social phenomena when we understand them in relation to their specific contexts and surrounding communities.

Details of research design

My primary approach to data collection was to establish a subtle yet constant presence at the museum and to interact with people in the museum's day-to-day practices. My interaction took various forms. I conducted formal interviews, including in-depth, open-ended, and group interviews, participant observations, and informal conversation with participants. I tried to follow the same participants throughout the three data collection periods, and I had more than 200 interviews in total over the entire study. My participants were connected to the museum and its community, including museum staff, board members, politicians, educators, community leaders, visitors, and non-visitors. I interviewed around 70 people each in 2011 and 2015, and 30 people in 2019. Additionally, I collected various documents and articles related to the history of the region as well as that of the museum, census data and other demographic information, and information related to the region's economic development. I also conducted visitor and non-visitor studies in 2015 and 2019.

To fully embrace the fact that the researcher and the research subject in an ethnographic study are inseparable, I took an active member position as a researcher (Adler and Adler 1994). I participated in the museum's variety of activities, such as meetings, programs, and special events within and outside the museum building (with the exception of those I was not allowed to attend such as the board's executive committee meetings). I tried to include all members of the museum, but some simply did not want to participate or never responded to my requests. I found it especially difficult to get meetings with board members. This created a boundary that I could not cross as an outside researcher. Despite these invisible boundaries, I intended to achieve a tone of being helpful, approachable, and professional at the museum. I believe most participants were comfortable talking to me or having me volunteer at events or talk to museum visitors.

Most of the staff members were open to me in terms of sharing their perspectives and opinions about the museum's practices and interactions among staff members, visitors, and other cultural organizations in the community. Some of them even anonymously shared interpersonal communication issues that were considered controversial. Overall, this informal approach allowed me to build a positive rapport with my participants, which resulted in their willingness to share their perspectives and ideas with me. Of course, some participants were more open than others, and some flat out said they did not want to talk to me, which I respected.

Data collection

I used different types of data collection methods in order to triangulate the collected data, and thereby, enhance the validity of the final report. Triangulation reduces the risk that the conclusions of a study reflect prejudices and personal biases from a single data collection method, source, or perspective (Maxwell 2013). I used interviews, direct participant observations, surveys, and other means including an unconventional method of walking to collect data. (This is not discussed here as I have published two articles about it elsewhere. See Jung 2014, 2018.)

INTERVIEWS

The majority of the collected data consisted of interview transcripts based on casual conversations, formal interviews, and group interviews. Interviewing is a useful research method for gaining access to unobservable aspects of participants' experience, such as their feelings and opinions (Dyson and Genishi 2005). I designed interview questions based on the guidelines by Glesne (2005). I was mindful of Glesne's advice to be aware of the relationship between research questions and interview questions. The purpose of interview questions is to find answers to the research questions, not directly transforming research questions into interview questions (Glesne 2005). Interview questions should be much more contextual and specific than research questions (Glesne 2005; Maxwell 2013).

Additionally, I tried to maintain a positive outlook and rapport with participants. It is imperative that the researcher develops a positive rapport between herself and participants in a desirable interview setting so that participants will feel comfortable sharing their ideas, thoughts, and experiences (Spradley 1979). "A basic sense of trust… allows for the free flow of information" (Spradley 1979, 78). I tried to build a sense of trust and comfort with my participants before posing interview questions. For example, I often opened an interview with warm-up questions by asking about their professional background. I also encouraged participants to ask me questions and to make comments at any time, to eliminate the possibility that they would feel interrogated.

I was consistent about asking the same core questions across all three data collection periods of 2011, 2015, and 2019 to be able to compare answers over time. When I needed additional insight on matters that were new since my previous visit, I simply added them rather than replacing existing ones.

OBSERVATIONS

Observation is "the fundamental base of all research methods" (Adler and Adler 1994, 389). In a qualitative and ethnographic study, researchers observe their subjects in their environment and do not attempt to manipulate or deliberately set up an experimentation that can change the participants' behaviors and, consequently, the results of the study (Adler and Adler 1994). One critical issue related to observation is the inherent subjectivity of the observer. What is observed in any research process is necessarily dependent on the researcher, the subjects, and the contextual circumstances (Angrosino 2005). Echoing the symbolic approach of knowing—interpretive epistemology that values multiple perspectives—a researcher cannot find one objective truth about a phenomenon under study because conflicting versions and interpretations are inevitable (Angrosino 2005).

Rather than seeing this as a liability of the method, ethnographic researchers must actively solicit participants' perspectives and interpretations so that phenomena can be seen and told from different perspectives (Angrosino 2005). To include and value as many perspectives as possible, researchers should strive for egalitarian participation from their participants as well as their active participation with them. For my study, I solicited as much feedback and involvement as possible from participants so that I could reevaluate my analysis and interpretations in light of their perspectives and avoid being blinded by personal biases or assumptions. For example, I reached out to all staff members regardless of their positions (e.g., the museum's security and restaurant staff). I also interviewed community members who have never been to the museum. I tried to experience the museum's various staff and committee meetings, programs, lectures, events, restaurant, gift shop, as well as that of the community by going to different parts of the region, talking to people in their environments, and simply walking around for observation and reflection.

VISITOR AND NON-VISITOR SURVEYS

After my first data collection at the museum in 2011, I realized that the museum did not have demographic information about its visitors and almost no information about non-visitors. To overcome this, I conducted a set of visitor and non-visitor studies each in 2015 and 2019. I used the museum's internal member, donor, and volunteer databases to send out a survey that included identical questions for both years. For visitor surveys, I received a total of 187 responses in 2015 and 375 responses in 2019. To get input from non-visitors, I used a local newspaper company who sent out my survey to its opt-in mailing list for a fee in both years. For non-visitor surveys, I saw a dramatic decrease in responses. I received a total of 218 responses in 2015 and 88 responses in 2019. Since the participants were random residents of the community and were not segmented by their usership of the museum, I ended up attracting a lot more visitors than non-visitors to these community-wide surveys, making the results almost identical to visitor studies. However, I included some of the qualitative responses collected from these community-wide surveys in the analysis.

OTHER MEANS OF DATA COLLECTION

I used photographs, sketches, and other visual diagrams to help reflect my understanding of the museum and its community. For example, photography is traditionally associated with the field of anthropology, where it historically was used to provide visual information for the classification of races and to support theories of social evolution (Harper 1994). While early use of photographic images in ethnography was understood to be capable of representing realistic, true depictions of the studied culture, photographs, like textual descriptions, are necessarily constructed and interpreted through the cultural and personal lens of the photographer and viewers (Harper 1994). I used photography mainly as a means of collecting visual information that could serve as a visual reminder of my observations. To protect confidentiality, I cannot share the photographs that show the obvious identity of the research site. However, they were used extensively as a way to enrich my written descriptions of the museum and the surrounding community.

Along with photographs, I incorporated visual mapping and drawing, some of which are included in this book to aid illustrations of abstract concepts, systems, and structures. Like the photographs, these served as reminders to me while I was writing up my findings, but they were also utilized as illustrations representing analysis in the reporting stage. These visual depictions provide readers an alternative means of making sense of analytic descriptions and interpretations. For example, by displaying the museum's organizational chart, readers can more easily understand my verbal explanation or description of the museum structure.

Data analysis and interpretation

Data analysis involves three interrelated processes: data reduction, data display, and conclusion drawing and verification (Huberman and Miles 1994). Data analysis in qualitative studies is an iterative process that does not have a clear ending. The initial step of data analysis is reading all of the collected data, such as interview transcripts or observational notes, while recording reflections and comments (Maxwell 2013). This can lead to developing tentative ideas about categories and relationships emerging from the information. This simple and substantial process of reading data and getting familiar with them can help researchers discover regularities, patterns, and significant topics in their data and select words and phrases to represent the emerging categories, patterns, and topics, which then become coding categories or units (Bogdan and Biklen 2002). This approach helps researchers reduce the amount of data and organize them by categories and topics, making them much more manageable and retrievable. I read and examined interview transcripts, recorded observations, and my research journal many times until I was able to discern emerging categories, themes, and patterns.

After I reduced the data and constructed my overarching categories and subcategories, I created a visual matrix of organizational, substantive, and theoretical categories as described by Maxwell (2013). Organizational categories are topics or themes of the study predetermined or emerged through data reduction; substantive categories are largely descriptive and are based on participants' interpretations of the phenomena; and theoretical categories place coded data through organizational and substantive categorizing in the context of theory or for development of theory from the researcher's perspective (Maxwell 2013). Organizational categories, or topics, became chapters and titles of subsections in this book, while substantive and theoretical categories were interwoven into each section to describe, explain, and interpret what I had collected, observed, and experienced in a thematic and theoretical manner. After I completed the initial matrix, I reread the data and displayed relevant data using bullet points of summaries, synopses, and quotes from participants forming preliminary chapters and subsections. Displayed rough data with categories and subcategories became the very first draft, which was no more than reduced raw data. Then, I coded the reduced and displayed data again using the themes from my matrix. In this process, I was able to identify further theoretical categories. Then, I started to form more elaborate patterns, interpretations, and arguments that were closely related to research questions and to the theoretical approach of the study. I followed this same process of data reduction, organization, and analyses for data collected from the three different times.

The final step was to identify meanings and draw conclusions. In other words, I re-analyzed my draft chapters further to achieve a more cohesive explanation and tighten my argument demonstrated by evidence, examples, existing literature, and theory. I re-coded this preliminary written report and shifted elements around to make the material textually and visually clearer and more coherent to readers. I repeated this process of "reworking" the material until I was satisfied with the organization of the book, results, arguments, and conclusions. Through the process of writing, revising, and editing, I continued to make changes in my interpretations and conclusions of the study.

Limitations of the methods and methodology

I recognize several limitations of my overall methodology, research methods, and design. This study is limited by (1) my subjectivity as a researcher, (2) the degree of openness of the participants, (3) the duration of data collection, (4) limited number and composition of participants, and (5) lack of generalizability.

First, as a human being, I cannot be free of assumptions and biases. The researcher collects and interprets differing views based on her own assumptions and biases. This is a limitation of a symbolic perspective, so it is important to reveal one's biases when writing up a qualitative research report. For example, I had preconceived notions about people in the Midwest who I thought to be conservative and somewhat racist. This is an unfair way to describe an entire region, although some people's attitude toward me reinforced this assumption, while others did not. While I tried to be as open as possible, no researcher can accurately and comprehensively represent the voice and perspective of every participant. There could be many different versions of what was happening at the Avery during the three time periods I was at the museum, and my interpretation is just one of the many versions based on differing perspectives.

I was concerned about how open museum staff members would be to an outsider they had never met prior to the commencement of the study. This was less of an issue for the second and third data collection periods. While most Avery staff members seemed open to me, the staff may have answered questions or behaved in ways that differed from usual to present a certain image. In addition, there were spaces where I was not allowed. For example, I was not allowed to attend the museum's executive board meetings, although I was permitted to sit in on other types of board and committee meetings.

The duration of the study could be a limitation as well. I felt that my stay of two months each time in 2011 and 2015 was sufficient to complete a comprehensive set of interviews and observations. The last visit for three weeks in 2019 was what I was able to do at the time, but it limited the amount of data that could be collected. These time frames were relatively short compared to the standpoint of traditional ethnographic research, which could take years of continuous observations. I acknowledge that the quality and characteristics of my data would have been different if I had devoted a longer time period to my research each time I visited the museum. My observations, therefore, reflect the exhibitions, programs, meetings, policies, and other changes that happened during the visits in three different periods. In any research project, the desire for the broadest data set possible must be balanced with issues of feasibility and the researcher's resource constraints.

Another limitation of the study is that I could not interview everybody in the community. I was able to interview nearly all staff members and about a third of board members (not across all three visits though). In addition, I did not talk to all visitors or non-visitors to the Avery, while I interviewed 20 of them in person. Visitor and non-visitor surveys supplemented some of these missing views. Another omission on my part was that I did not notice until my second visit that I did not intentionally seek to get input from people of color and of different socioeconomic backgrounds. This goes back to my subjectivity as a human being who must work hard to see what she is not seeing. I fixed this for my second and third visits, but still most of my participants ended up being white, wealthy, and better educated than the overall community population. I acknowledge that not being fully inclusive of diverse and differing perspectives limits my understanding of the museum in relation to its broader community.

Lastly, the study does not generalize in the sense of quantitative research. In qualitative research, generalization can happen by readers who can interpret my study in different ways and apply their understanding to the specific practices of their own unique situations. In this process, readers make various interpretations and naturalistic generalizations (Stake 1995). My intent was that my analysis could generate a theoretical yet practical model that staff members and professionals from comparable organizations can find helpful as they seek ways to transform their practices. Additionally, the museum's location and its external context make this book US-centric. While the specificity and contextual information is about the United States, the similarities and analysis can be used for other museums in other countries through naturalistic generalizations.

References

AAM (American Alliance of Museums). 2018. *Facing Change: Insights from the American Alliance of Museums' Diversity, Equity, Accessibility, and Inclusion Working Group*. Arlington, VA: American Alliance of Museums. https://www.aam-us.org/wp-content/uploads/2018/04/AAM-DEAI-Working-Group-Full-Report-2018.pdf.

Adler, P. A., and P. Adler. 1994. "Observational Techniques." In *The Sage Handbook of Qualitative Research*, 1st ed., edited by N. K. Denzin and Y. S. Lincoln, 337–392. Thousand Oaks, CA: Sage Publications.

Anderson, M. 2020. "Art Museums in the Pandemic." *Art Law Podcast*, May 11, 2020. http://artlawpodcast.com/2020/05/11/art-museums-in-the-pandemic/.

Angrosino, M. 2005. "Recontextualizing Observation: Ethnography, Pedagogy, and the Prospects for a Progressive Political Agenda." In *The Sage Handbook of Qualitative Research*, 3rd ed., edited by N. K. Denzin and Y. S. Lincoln, 729–745. Thousand Oaks, CA: Sage Publications.

Association of Art Museums Directors. 2018. *Art Museums by the Numbers 2018*. https://aamd.org/sites/default/files/document/Art%20Museums%20by%20the%20Numbers%202018.pdf.

Bate, S. P. 1997. "Whatever Happened to Organizational Anthropology? A Review of the Field of Organizational Ethnography and Anthropological Studies." *Human Relations* 50 (9): 1147–1175. https://doi.org/10.1177/001872679705000905.

Bergeron, A., and B. Tuttle. 2013. *Magnetic: The Art and Science of Engagement.* Washington, DC: American Alliance of Museums.

Bogdan, R. C., and S. K. Biklen. 2002. *Qualitative Research for Education: An Introduction to Theory and Methods.* 4th ed. Boston, MA: Allyn and Bacon.

Boucher, B. 2020. "People Are Calling for Museums to Be Abolished. Can Whitewashed American History Be Rewritten?" *CNN (website).* Last modified July 12, 2020. https://www.cnn.com/style/article/natural-history-museum-whitewashing-monuments-statues-trnd/index.html.

Dyson, A. H., and C. Genishi. 2005. *On the Case: Approaches to Language and Literacy Research.* New York: Teachers College Press.

Falk, J. H., and B. K. Sheppard. 2006. *Thriving in the Knowledge Age: New Business Models for Museums and Other Cultural Institutions.* Lanham, MD: Altamira Press.

Geertz, C. 1973. *The Interpretation of Cultures.* New York: Basic Books.

Glesne, C. 2005. *Becoming Qualitative Researchers: An Introduction.* 3rd ed. Boston, MA: Allyn and Bacon.

Hammersley, M., and P. Atkinson. 2007. *Ethnography: Principles in Practice.* New York: Routledge.

Harper, D. 1994. "On the Authority of the Image: Visual Methods at the Crossroads." In *The Sage Handbook of Qualitative Research*, 1st ed., edited by N. K. Denzin and Y. S. Lincoln, 118–137. Thousand Oaks, CA: Sage Publications.

Hatch, M. J. 2018. *Organization Theory: Modern, Symbolic, and Postmodern Perspectives.* 4th ed. Oxford: Oxford University Press.

Huberman, A. M., and M. B. Miles. 1994. "Data Management and Analysis Methods." In *The Sage Handbook of Qualitative Research*, 1st ed., edited by N. K. Denzin and Y. S. Lincoln, 428–444. Thousand Oaks, CA: Sage Publications.

Janes, R. R., and R. Sandell, eds. 2019. *Museum Activism.* Abingdon: Routledge.

Jung, Y. 2014. "Mindful Walking: The Serendipitous Journey of Community-based Ethnography." *Qualitative Inquiry* 20 (5): 621–627. https://doi.org/10.1177/1077800413505543.

Jung, Y. 2018. "Mindful Walking: Transforming Distant Web of Social Connections into Active Qualitative Empirical Materials from a Postmodern Flâneuse's Perspective." In *The Flâneur and Education Research. Palgrave Studies in Movement across Education, the Arts and the Social Sciences*, edited by A. L. Cutcher and R. Irwin, 113–130. Cham: Palgrave Pivot. https://doi.org/10.1007/978-3-319-72838-4_5.

Lord, G. D., and N. Blankenberg. 2015. *Cities, Museums, and Soft Power.* Washington, DC: American Alliance of Museums.

MacLeod, J. 2009. *Ain't No Makin' It: Aspirations and Attainment in a Low-Income Neighborhood.* 3rd ed. Boulder, CO: Westview Press.

Maxwell, J. A. 2013. *Qualitative Research Design: An Interactive Approach.* 3rd ed. Thousand Oaks, CA: Sage Publications.

Merriam, S. B. 2002. "Introduction to Qualitative Research." In *Qualitative Research in Practice: Examples for Discussion and Analysis*, edited by S. B. Merriam, 3–17. San Francisco: Jossey-Bass.

Metropolitan Museum of Art. 2019. *2018 990 Form.* https://www.metmuseum.org/-/media/files/about-the-met/990-forms/2018-irs-form-990-for-fy2019.pdf.

Moore, K. 1994. "Introduction: Museum Management." In *Museums Management*, edited by K. Moore, 1–14. London: Routledge.

Spradley, J. P. 1979. *The Ethnographic Interview.* New York: Holt, Rinehart and Winston.

Stake, R. E. 1995. *The Art of Case Study Research.* Thousand Oaks, CA: Sage Publications.

Tedlock, B. 2000. "Ethnography and Ethnographic Representation." In *The Sage Handbook of Qualitative Research*, 2nd ed., edited by N. K. Denzin and Y. S. Lincoln, 455–486. Thousand Oaks, CA: Sage Publications.

Tørring, B., J. H. Gittell, M. Laursen, B. S. Rasmussen and E. E. Sørensen. 2019. "Communication and Relationship Dynamics in Surgical Teams in the Operating Room: An Ethnographic Study." *BMC Health Services Research* 19: 528. https://doi.org/10.1186/s12913-019-4362-0.

Whyte, W. 1969. *Organizational Behaviour: Theory and Application.* Homewood, IL: Richard D. Irwin.

Wolcott, H. F. 2008. *Ethnography: A Way of Seeing.* Lanham, MD: AltaMira Press.

2 Open systems theory and mutual causality

Brief introduction to organization theories in museums

Museums have long followed a traditional, compartmentalized, and hierarchical organizational structure. Low (1942) noted that curatorial and educational roles are organized into different departments with curatorial usually at the top of a museum hierarchy. He identified this top-down hierarchical and compartmentalized museum structure in the mid-twentieth century as an obstacle toward becoming a social instrument that fosters civic engagement (Low 1942), yet it still is reflected in today's museum structure (Janes and Sandell 2019). This organizational structure does not provide a systemic way to get different ideas and perspectives from all parts of a museum and its community. This mechanical museum structure is aligned with the modernist organization theories. For instance, Taylor's (1911) scientific management theory and Weber's (1964) bureaucracy influenced the dominant museum management theories being operated as a hierarchical and bureaucratic institution with a lone director in charge of major decision-making (Janes and Sandell 2019; Moore 1994).

Recognizing these classic organization theories often neglected how humanistic factors and relationships influenced organizational effectiveness, more recent museum management approaches are based on humanistic organizational theories. Adopting behavioral science to understand organizations, human resource-related organization theories emphasize how organizations and the people who run them grow and develop in relation to each other. This shift shows a movement toward a model reflecting more interdependence between organizations and people and valuing the roles and behaviors of people in affecting organizational effectiveness and outcomes (Shafritz, Ott, and Jang 2016). In this view, people are not parts of a machine. Rather, they create a cooperative community made of complex human relationships (Handy 1993). In the past couple of decades, more museums and professionals are moving toward soft management and organic organizational models that value networks of ideas and people-centered approaches rather than traditional hierarchies and object-centered practices (Bergeron and Tuttle 2013; Janes 2009; Lord and Blankenberg 2015; Moore 1994).

Open systems theory embraces the human relations approach yet develops it further to be more inclusive of different parts of the community, or the external environment. While humanistic organization theories acknowledge the influence of the environment on organizations, they focus more on the organizational units and their components, such as people within them, not considering environments as important parts and units of analysis in understanding organizations (Scott and Davis 2007; Sharfitz, Ott, and Jang 2016). In open systems theory, the environment is not only an important part of analysis in understanding an organization, but an organization and its environment alter each other situated within a mutually interconnected reality. In other words, an organization influences its environment by interacting with it, while the environment influences the organization's internal systems and helps define what it is.

Why open systems theory?

Open systems theory, at a macro level, brings a different perspective to the mechanical and humanistic tradition of museum management, critiquing and offering different ways of managing and organizing museums. Applying and expanding on understanding museums through this lens would influence the outcome of what they can do for their communities as they are (or should be) an integral part of the community. Open systems theory offers a way to look at not only the parts but their interrelationships and how they are connected to their communities (Jung and Vakharia 2019).

This open systems idea is especially important for museums for two reasons. First, traditionally museums have had a narrow and exclusive connection to their environment. For example, museums have served a small portion of the overall population who tend to be white, wealthy, and well educated (Dana 1917; Farrell and Medvedeva 2010; Fleming 2002). While this exclusive practice has been under scrutiny for years, museums were called on to make more profound and urgent changes with the new wave of the civil rights movement in the United States which occurred concurrently with and was triggered by the unprecedented COVID-19 pandemic in 2020 (Dafoe and Goldstein 2020). During these triple challenges of the pandemic, economic distress, and civil unrest, many museums let go of their most vulnerable and diverse staff members who tend to be at the bottom of the museum hierarchy rather than sharing the burden (Anderson 2020). Some have questioned if museums should continue in their current form and practice, while others asked for a complete abolishment of museums (Boucher 2020). The practice of disenfranchising the most vulnerable group in the museum ranks reveals the internal and somewhat hidden museum core and their priority, and stresses the need for a structural change, not just lip service or token efforts. One notable movement pushing museums toward sustainable changes is called "Death to Museums." Emerging museum professionals and scholars created and organized this movement, which has a manifesto, monthly meetings, and symposiums. Its website states (Death to Museums 2020), we challenge the idea of returning to "normal" once the pandemic ends when "normal" means inequality, instability, extremely low wages, and an embarrassing lack of diversity across museum staff. Instead, we want to harness the collective potential of museum workers working towards radical change.

Second, the role and rationale of museums in the United States highlight how museums should be more integrated into their community not only in their physical presence but also in their missions, roles, and activities that should be useful for their wider communities. One distinctive structure of US museums is that they are mostly private nonprofits. They are exempt from paying federal income taxes, as well as exempt from paying most state taxes. Additionally, people who donate to museums get a tax deduction on their donation, essentially getting the portion of money back equivalent to their income tax rate if they itemize the donation when they file taxes. These perks are given to nonprofit museums and their patrons because museums are supposed to benefit the wider public through their educational mission. To be tax-exempt organizations, they must have a purpose that is worthy of this benefit, which can be seen as a built-in government subsidy. While there are several tax-exempt purposes, museums squarely fall under the purpose of education (IRS 2020). The purpose of a museum, therefore, is legally to educate the public as a whole, not just the typical museum goers who are white, wealthy, and highly educated. It is their obligation to offer diverse services, be inclusive, and provide relevant education that is truly needed by their communities at their entirety (Jung 2015).

While there have been some discussions on systems theory in the museum field (Fopp 1997; Jung 2011; Latham and Simmons 2014), these are rather theoretical and lack practical applicability. Recognizing this gap, my co-editor, Ann Rowson Love, and I edited a book titled *Systems Thinking in Museums: Theory and Practice* (2017). This book explains the general understanding of open systems theory applied to museums and then introduces examples of international museum practices that utilize systems theory or thinking in many different areas of museum operation such as leadership, exhibition installation, and financial management. This edited book was one of the most comprehensive attempts in introducing open systems theory into the field of museums. The current book develops this theory even further, making it more specific and contextualized based on a thorough analysis of long-term data of a real museum practice over an eight-year time span.

Open systems perspective: organizations and their environments

General systems theorist Ludwig von Bertalanffy (1933, 1972) first developed an open systems theory that pays attention to interdependence between parts in an attempt to understand the whole, rather than dissecting and studying each part separately. Von Bertalanffy (1933, 64) wrote, "Since the fundamental character of the living thing is its organization, the customary investigation of the single parts and processes... cannot provide a complete explanation of the vital phenomena." Parts are nested in a layered and networked structure and cannot exist independently from each other and without the whole. For example, a person as a system of itself is part of an organization, a social system. An organization is a part of its larger community, which is part of a larger society, country, and the rest of the world. Additionally, all of these subsystems, systems, and suprasystems are parts of the natural ecosystem. Thus, interconnected and interdependent realities among human beings, species, organizations, societies, and natural ecosystems form a web of life (Bateson 2000; Capra 1996) that is not escapable. These interconnections among different types and levels of parts and systems, *in relation to each other* and *with their environment*, make them *open* systems. Some important characteristics of open social systems are that they are flexible and adaptable, they exist in some sort of networked hierarchy, and they stabilize or renew themselves through feedback functions.

Recognizing different types and levels of systems could help explain social organizations as open systems that are flexible and adaptable. In mechanistic systems (e.g., a machine), the parts behave in a certain order that is highly constrained and limited, making it more of a closed system, which is not affected by changes in its external environment (Scott and Davis 2007). In organic systems (e.g., a plant or animal), the parts are more interdependent and less constrained with more flexibility and adaptability for change; they are open systems making changes internally based on the input received from their external environment (Scott and Davis 2007). In social systems, like organizations and museums, independent parts are loosely connected with fewer constraints and limitations, characterized as complex and flexible open systems (Scott and Davis 2007). Organizations and social systems, including units, groups, and individuals, are loosely connected to each other and are capable of independent actions while being interdependent (Ashby 1952). These flexible moving parts make it possible for organizations to be more adaptive for the system as a whole in relation to its external environment.

Another critical element of open systems is networked hierarchy. While one may think of hierarchy as rigid and ranked power differences reflected in organizations, it is an important feature of complex open systems and a mechanism of clustering (Scott and Davis 2007). The concept of hierarchy from an open systems perspective is more like a tree root or holarchy, which helps understand open systems as composed of networked and layered structures (Macy 1991). For example, all systems have subsystems; to understand the system, one must understand its external larger systems and subsystems as well as interconnections among all the layers (Scott and Davis 2007). This way of examining organizations is different from reductionism, which is the primary method used by most modernist organization theorists.

"Reductionism generates knowledge and understanding of phenomena by breaking them down into constituent parts and then studying these simple elements in terms of cause and effect" (Flood 2010, 269), missing the effects of interconnections, mutual casualty, and nuanced and complex understanding of organizations. A holistic way of looking at organizations factors in the effect of the environment, understanding organizations or social systems as interconnected and as parts of larger environments (Schwab 1960).

Because open systems fully acknowledge the effect and interaction between organizations and their external environment, they can maintain themselves based on inputs of resources or information from the environment (Scott and Davis 2007). This feedback mechanism of an open system receives inputs from the external environment and transforms them into useful outputs for their environment by its internal throughput process. When a social system does not transform or change itself based on the input from the environment, it may merely survive by maintaining its status quo but cannot renew itself to become a continued meaningful part of its environment. This interplay of feedback functions of an open system is essential in transforming a system over time and is further explored below.

Open systems theory and mutual causality of Buddhism

Although the early general systems theory in the Western world is attributed to the work of von Bertalanffy, systems thinking nested in mutual belonging is ancient (Macy 1991). Macy (1991) compares the general systems theory to that of early teachings of Buddhism. Based on early Buddhist teachings, the idea of *self* is not a fixed, isolated being; rather, it is a flexible and changing construct that the dynamics of the mind create (Macy 1991). These flexible and mutable beings, or a collective of selves, coexist in profound mutual belonging and interdependence (Macy 1991). Naess (1973), using the concept of *deep ecology*, explains this fundamental, unescapable mutual interconnection and interdependence among all parts of the natural ecosystem regardless how small they may be. These ideas of deep ecology and mutual belonging are also reflected in Bateson's (2000) *Ecology of Mind* that sees the human mind as immanent not only in the body but also in surrounding environments including systems of human relationships, the society, or the natural ecosystem. This thinking disrupts the mind and body as well as human and nature dichotomy, challenging the dominant Cartesian thought of putting human intelligence separate from and above its natural surroundings (Bowers 1993).

Macy (1991, 1) defined mutual causality as "dynamic interdependence where phenomena affect each other in a reciprocal or mutual fashion." The Buddha's teaching of causality is called *paticca samuppada*, meaning conditionality or relativity or dependent co-arising (Macy 1991). The mutual causality in this sense is conditional like *if* and *when* rather than *because* (Macy 1991). Mutual causality is one of the most important concepts of both systems theory and the teachings of Buddhism. It is different from linear and unidirectional causality from the positivist perspective, which expects to have a predictable and mechanistic process and result. Based on the concept of mutual causality, an open system is a non-summative whole, which cannot be reduced to its parts (Macy 1991; von Bertalanffy 1972). An open system is not only a whole on its own but also part of a larger whole (Macy 1991). In this nested interconnected structure of a subsystem within a larger system, the external system is integral and co-determinative in maintaining and renewing the subsystem, leading to mutual adaptations (Macy 1991).

A museum is a non-summative whole and cannot be reduced to its collection, one department, or programs. It exists dependent on the interaction and interdependence caused by all actors, things, and parts of the museum. A museum, an open and whole system, is also nested within its community, the larger open system. Without the inputs, such as information, resources, people, and visitors, from the community, the museum cannot exist. The changes happening in the external environment affect the museum to resist or adapt to change. The museum also provides outputs to the community, for example, providing educational and entertainment opportunities. It could even alter the internal practice of other organizations that coexist within their larger community. For instance, the museum could lobby to get public funding from its local government which could alter the government's goals or values in supporting that funding. Or the museum could embark on private-public partnership in providing more afterschool education for local schools. Therefore, the museum, the larger whole of the community, and other organizations in the community are integral and co-determinative in maintaining and renewing each other.

Negative and positive feedback functions

An open system is self-stabilizing through negative feedback processes, adjusting its output to match the input and internal codes or values (Macy 1991). The negative feedback function can also be explained by the processes of *morphostasis* that help maintain a system's given form or state, such as circulation and respiration in biological systems and socialization and control activities in social systems (Scott and Davis 2007). In this negative feedback process, mental percepts of incoming data of the external interaction match internal codes, values, or goals (Macy 1991). In this case, the incoming data seem meaningful to internal actors' existing constructs or mental models (i.e., status quo assumptions and thought processes behind the way actors have performed their previous work) encouraging them to continue perpetuating this match, maintaining the status quo of what has worked and what has been meaningful to them. Through the negative feedback mechanism, an organization stabilizes itself, making sense of the world (Macy 1991). Museums have long maintained this negative feedback function, stabilizing themselves through producing exhibitions and programs (outputs) that match the needs and contributions of existing donors and patrons. They continuously and incrementally adjust their internal goals, codes, or mental models of the museum to meet the needs and wants of existing donors and patrons. With this negative feedback process, museums maintain the status quo, adjusting its "output to minimize the disparity between input and code" (Macy 1991, 98). Self-stabilizing is an important function of an open system, but it can deter organizations from seeing the need for fundamental change that is necessary for growth, learning, adaptation, and renewal.

An open system is self-organizing. This self-organization or positive feedback process can be explained using the concept of *morphogenesis*, which describes a process of changing the system such as learning, growing, and differentiating (Scott and Davis 2007). This happens when a system experiences a mismatch between incoming information and internal pattern, structure, code, or mental models (Macy 1991). To process that new information, the system creates new throughputs adopting a new culture, structure, and coding or interpretive system (Macy 1991). Successfully incorporating positive feedback can lead to differentiation and complexification of internal structure (Macy 1991). In other words, a positive feedback process leads to deviation as it cannot minimize the mismatch between percepts and pre-established internal code, pattern, or model (Macy 1991). This complex and more vulnerable structure is subject to disorganization yet gains a greater flexibility to adapt, be more responsive to, and be able to process external changes (Macy 1991). Museums also adopt the positive feedback function. For example, some museums have seen that they could not attract certain groups of people from their communities exacerbated by the shrinking group of traditional museum goers due to changing demographics. In this situation, museums can reorganize themselves to find a new pattern or goals to respond to this mismatch by finding different and complex ways to get more diverse input to attract nontraditional patrons and visitors. Some museums reinvented themselves to be worthy of broader support by offering new programs, diversifying their permanent collections, hiring more people of color and of different backgrounds, and changing the funding structure so they would not rely on a small group of donors that is disappearing.

As summarized in Figure 2.1, while open systems maintain and stabilize (i.e., morphostasis) themselves through a negative feedback loop, they differentiate (i.e., morphogenesis) themselves from others and adopt a more elaborate and complex structure by learning to change in relation to their external environment. This leads to modifying and restructuring internal mental models, and the organizational system gets more complicated and moves toward "greater improbability and variety" (Macy 1991, 74). All the elements of the loop are interdependent, affecting each other in a multi-directional way as indicated in the double-sided arrows shown in Figure 2.1.

A feedback loop is an important mechanism in mutual causality because the mechanism enables inaction or transformational change. Effects of actions are fed back to the organization making the internal organization and

Open systems theory and mutual causality

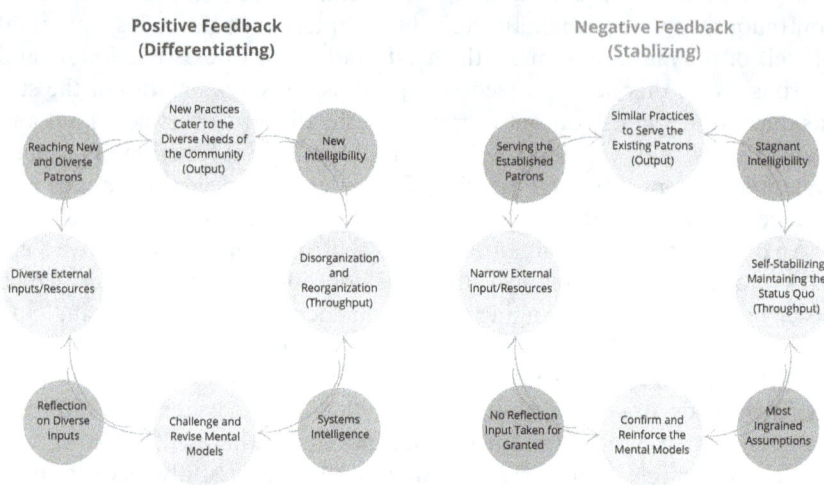

Figure 2.1 Open Systems Organization and Its Feedback Functions.

its actions inter-determinative or mutually affecting (Macy 1991). Negative feedback reinforces the status quo by reducing deviations between goals (based on limited inputs) and performance of the internal systems and outputs; positive feedback encourages the deviations leading to changes, creating novelty and instability in the internal systems and outputs. Through a positive feedback process, transformational changes happen. When a positive feedback process is well leveraged, an organization can maintain the state of dynamic equilibrium, balancing itself with the tension between the forces that build up and break down its components (Macy 1991). Dynamic equilibrium refers to a state where a constant change is happening in relation to external pressures in an effort to be relevant (von Bertalanffy 1950). It is distinctive from a stale equilibrium, maintaining the status quo found in an organization that perpetuates negative feedback processes, or from a complete chaos that may break down the entire system. A system in a dynamic equilibrium remains flexible and complex and prepared to respond to any emerging challenges and opportunities (Jung 2017). "Like the tightrope walker who must raise her eyes to keep her balance, the system maintains its dynamic equilibrium by looking ahead" (Macy 1991, 85).

Mental models, systems intelligence, and new intelligibility

When the mental models of actors are fixed and based on past experiences and practices only, it is difficult to get out of a negative feedback loop. Mental models are people's taken-for-granted beliefs and assumptions which affect how they think, talk, and act (Kania, Kramer, and Senge 2018). These mental models are often the basis for many "isms" people display such as racism, sexism, ageism, and ableism (Kania, Kramer, and Senge 2018). When these mental models are fixed, the chances of seeing the need for change are slim as individuals and organizations would only see the information that confirms and reinforces their existing belief system. Laszlo explains how this negative feedback function allows one to live in the "assumed form-world" evolved from one's past experiences or fixed mental models (Laszlo 1972, 128). If we are only willing to see the world based on our own past experiences and pay attention only to those that confirm and reinforce the existing assumptions and beliefs, transformational change would not occur (Laszlo 1972). Like mind and body are inseparable, an organization's mental models are inseparable from its overarching culture and structure. Mental models are reflected in how an organization is run, and in turn the overarching structure influences the mental models of the organization and those of the actors, constantly reinforcing and affirming each other. This can change by deliberately and critically examining the organization's mental models as well as explicit structure of practices and policies for a sustainable and transformational change (Kania, Kramer, and Senge 2018). To revise the dominant and status quo mental models, an organization should engage in a positive feedback loop, and in the process, it can achieve new intelligibility making the system more open and vulnerable (Macy 1991).

To change the mental models that maintain the status quo, the concept of systems intelligence is key. Based on the work of Senge's (1990) systems thinking perspective and Goleman's (1998) notion of emotional intelligence, systems intelligence refers to the intelligence behind an action that is taken after a careful consideration of one's position within a complex system (Saarinen and Hämäläinen 2004). Systems intelligence is similar to systems thinking (Senge 1990), which is a way of thinking about the world or any phenomena where its parts are interconnected to and interdependent with each other and situated within the larger whole. Based on this foundation, systems intelligence focuses more on one's thinking behind his or her action to deliberately alter the thinking and therefore their behavior. Some of the qualities of a systems intelligent person are that she understands she is a part of a larger system, manages her behavior in relation to the external environment, understands how other people behave and how her action affects their behavior, and works with others to improve the larger environment she is part of (Törmänen, Hämäläinen, and Saarinen 2016). With this keen understanding of one's presence and relationship with the larger system, the actors behave openly and with sensitivity (Hämäläinen and Saarinen 2007). Systems intelligence has a potential to alter one's mental models by adjusting to the changes and effects of the larger system and thus leading to sustainable micro-behavioral changes affecting the whole system (Sasaki 2017).

Systems intelligence is something that should be embraced by all actors of a system. However, its largest impact can be felt in the leadership level, creating and promoting the learning organization environment (Keeney and Jung 2018). In an effective learning organization, actors learn to become more systems intelligent by listening to each other, challenging the status quo assumptions together, acting in accordance with transformed thoughts (Törmänen, Hämäläinen, and Saarinen 2016), and thus maintaining the positive feedback mechanism for an organization to renew and transform. System leaders see the larger system of which they are a part, look at a big picture of how a problem is related to different parts of the system, and come up with a systemic solution that can address the foundation of the issue rather than just the symptoms as manifested on surface levels (Senge, Hamilton, and Kania 2015). This approach prohibits actors of a system from engaging in short-term and reactive problem-solving practices. System leadership also values the time and space for reflection and generative conversation to hear differing views among actors from many parts of the system (Senge, Hamilton, and Kania 2015). Systems intelligent leaders and involved actors can slow down and try on different viewpoints in solving problems through collective creativity and challenging deeply ingrained assumptions ultimately transforming "relationships among people who shape those systems" (Senge, Hamilton, and Kania 2015). When a system leader encourages and promotes a learning environment and all actors embrace systems intelligence, they collectively and continuously adjust their percepts and actions, adapting and reorganizing internal systems and their mental models to meet the changing needs of the external system. It is the exploratory and learning behaviors embraced by the actors of the system that transform their system to reach new intelligibility as a collective whole and become a learning organization that leads to external transformation and social change (Macy 1991).

Toward paradigm shift

This collective intelligibility of actors, not disparate individual efforts, can lead to true, long-lasting transformation, ultimately shifting a paradigm of the field. A paradigm describes the mental context where problems arise and are resolved (Macy 1991). Often an issue or problem is raised and addressed using a strategy that has worked in the past which justifies and maintains the existing paradigm of a place. When new issues arise that are no longer possible to be resolved from the existing mental context, inadequacy of the paradigm assumptions or mental models is raised (Kuhn 1962; Macy 1991). Thus, the assumptions of linear causation that things are predictable, mechanistic, and will lead to some sort of explainable answer every time would not lead to a paradigm shift (Macy 1991) that requires challenging and revising that very mental model the problem arises from. "A genuine understanding of mutual causality involves a transcendence of conventional dichotomies between self and world, a transformation of the way experience is processed, which amounts to an overhauling of one's most ingrained assumptions" (Macy 1991, 19). As I discussed above, these stubborn assumptions are called mental models and can be altered through systems intelligence that can enable the positive feedback process toward greater diversity, variety, and ultimately renewed organization. When these are applied to field-wide museum practices, a paradigm shift of the museum field is possible challenging what has been an accepted and standard practice and adopting new and relevant practice that could be the "new" industry norm until the next paradigm arrives out of necessity due to changing realities.

A good example of a process of paradigm shift can be found in the controversy involving the planned retrospective exhibition of Philip Guston entitled *Philip Guston Now*. Guston was an influential Jewish American artist whose work speaks to and challenges the concepts of white supremacy and anti-semitism apparent in his imagery of hooded Klansmen. Initially scheduled to open in 2020, the organizing museums—the National Gallery of Art in Washington, DC; the Tate Modern in London; the Museum of Fine Arts, Boston; and the Museum of Fine Arts, Houston—decided to postpone the exhibition until 2024 under the pressure of civil unrest and museums being called out for their troublesome history of racism and elitism (Farago 2020; McGlone and Smee 2020). Some of the rationale for this postponement was that they were not prepared to embark on such important work in an appropriate way and not offend any audiences (McGlone and Smee 2020). This action of postponement of such an important exhibition triggered many artists, critics, curators, and scholars to write an open letter to these institutions and demanded the reinstatement of the exhibition, rather than detracting from it in the fear of not getting it right. The open letter (*Brooklyn Rail*, 2020) said that these institutions' action publicly manifested "their longstanding failure to have educated, integrated, and prepared themselves to meet the challenge of the renewed pressure for racial justice." One of the museums acknowledged that the exhibition planning team originally did not include any black curators stating, "I am concerned we can't do this show without having an African American curator as part of the project" (Feldman, National Gallery of Art Director, quoted in McGlone and Smee 2020). This adds evidence of these museums not prepared internally to take on such challenges, triggering a positive feedback function toward meeting the new challenges by transforming themselves. These museums' reactive response to postpone the exhibition could be their mental models acting in accordance with previous field-wide practice of avoiding issues rather than confronting them.

When the external environment changes and the existing practice of museums is no longer acceptable, they must find ways to meet the new challenge by transforming themselves internally. They cannot solve a problem based on the old mental model that created the problem in the first place. More recent development of this issue at the end of 2020 indicates that the exhibition has been reinstated and plans to open in 2022 (Cascone 2020). This is a perfect condition for paradigm shift to happen—a mismatch between internal practice and external pressure. Museums' failure to deal with an external and complex issue backfired indicating that the old way of doing things is no longer working, showing the mismatch between the input and mental models or throughputs of internal structure and culture. By utilizing a positive feedback function and applying it to the museum-wide and field-wide practice, museums can close this mismatch transforming their internal structure and mental models to meet the external needs and pressures.

In order to present outputs that match the new pressure, challenges, and expectations, museums must transform their internal culture and structure by challenging the mental models of actors and trying on different ideas from new and necessary voices (i.e., new inputs). This book attempts to show how museums can trigger more positive feedback functions that can lead to a field-wide paradigm shift to meet the changing needs, interests, and pressures of the new realities.

References

Anderson, M. 2020. "Art Museums in the Pandemic." *Art Law Podcast*, May 11, 2020. http://artlawpodcast.com/2020/05/11/art-museums-in-the-pandemic/.
Ashby, W. R. 1952. *A Design for a Brain*. New York: John Wiley.
Bateson, G. 2000. *Steps to an Ecology of Mind*. Chicago: University of Chicago Press.
Bergeron, A., and B. Tuttle. 2013. *Magnetic: The Art and Science of Engagement*. Washington, DC: American Alliance of Museums.
Boucher, B. 2020. "People Are Calling for Museums to Be Abolished. Can Whitewashed American History Be Rewritten?" *CNN (website)*. Last modified July 12, 2020. https://www.cnn.com/style/article/natural-history-museum-whitewashing-monuments-statues-trnd/index.html.
Bowers, C. A. 1993. *Critical Essays on Education, Modernity, and the Recovery of the Ecological Imperative*. New York: Teachers College Press.
Brooklyn Rail. 2020. "Open Letter: On Philip Guston Now." September 30, 2020. https://brooklynrail.org/projects/on-philip-guston-now/.
Capra, F. 1996. *The Web of Life: A New Scientific Understanding of Living Systems*. New York: Anchor Books.
Cascone, S. 2020. "The Postponed Philip Guston Show Will Now Open in 2022 With New Contributions From Artists and Historians." *Artnet News*, November 5, 2020. https://news.artnet.com/exhibitions/postponed-philip-guston-show-will-now-open-2022-museums-say-1919119.
Dafoe, T., and C. Goldstein. 2020. "The George Floyd Protests Spurred Museums to Promise Change. Here's What They've Actually Done So Far." *Artnet News*, August 14, 2020. https://news.artnet.com/art-world/museums-diversity-equity-commitments-1901564.
Dana, J. C. 1917. *The New Museum*. Woodstock, VT: The Elm Tree Press.
Death to Museums. n.d. "Death to Museums." (website). Accessed November 9, 2020. https://deathtomuseums.com/.
Farago, J. 2020. "The Philip Guston Show Should Be Reinstated." *New York Times*, September 30, 2020. https://www.nytimes.com/2020/09/30/arts/design/philip-guston-shows-open-letter.html.

Farrell, B., and M. Medvedeva. 2010. *Demographic Transformation and the Future of Museums*. Washington, DC: American Association of Museums.

Fleming, D. 2002. "Positioning the Museum for Social Inclusion." In *Museums, Society, Inequality*, edited by R. Sandell, 213–224. New York: Routledge.

Flood, R. L. 2010. "The Relationship of 'Systems Thinking' to Action Research." *Systemic Practice and Action Research* 23 (4): 269–284.

Fopp, M. A. 1997. *Managing Museums and Galleries*. London: Routledge.

Goleman, D. 1998. *Working with Emotional Intelligence*. New York: Bantam.

Hämäläinen, R. P., and E. Saarinen. 2007. "Systems Intelligence: A Key Competence in Human Action and Organizational Life." In *Systems Intelligence in Leadership and Everyday Life*, edited by R. Hämäläinen and E. Saarinen, 39–50. Helsinki: Helsinki University of Technology.

Handy, C. 1993. *Understanding Organizations: How Understanding the Ways Organizations Actually Work Can Be Used to Manage Them Better*. New York: Oxford University Press.

IRS (Internal Revenue Service). 2020. "Exempt Purposes - Internal Revenue Code Section 501(c)(3)." *Charitable Organizations*. Last modified July 28, 2020. https://www.irs.gov/charities-non-profits/charitable-organizations/exempt-purposes-internal-revenue-code-section-501c3.

Janes, R. R. 2009. *Museums in a Troubled World: Renewal, Irrelevance or Collapse?* New York: Routledge.

Janes, R. R., and R. Sandell, eds. 2019. *Museum Activism*. Abingdon: Routledge.

Jung, Y. 2011. "The Art Museum Ecosystem: A New Alternative Model." *Museum Management and Curatorship* 26 (4): 321–338. https://doi.org/10.1080/09647775.2011.603927.

Jung, Y. 2015. "Diversity Matters: Theoretical Understanding of and Suggestions for the Current Fundraising Practices of Nonprofit Art Museums." *The Journal of Arts Management, Law, and Society* 45 (4): 255–268. https://doi.org/10.1080/10632921.2015.1103672.

Jung, Y. 2017. "Toward a Learning Museum and Systems Intelligence." In *Systems Thinking in Museums: Theory and Practice*, edited by Y. Jung and A. R. Love, 229–234. Lanham, MD: Rowman and Littlefield.

Jung, Y., and A. R. Love, eds. 2017. *Systems Thinking in Museums: Theory and Practice*. Lanham, MD: Rowman and Littlefield.

Jung, Y., and N. Vakharia. 2019. "Open Systems Theory for Arts and Cultural Organizations: Linking Structure and Performance." *The Journal of Arts Management, Law, and Society* 49 (4): 257–273. https://doi.org/10.1080/10632921.2019.1617813.

Kania, J., M. Kramer, and P. Senge. 2018. *The Water of Systems Change*. Seattle, WA: FSG. https://www.fsg.org/publications/water_of_systems_change.

Keeney, K. P., and Y. Jung. 2018. "Global Arts Leadership: An Exploration of Professional Standards and Demands in Arts Management." *The Journal of Arts Management, Law, and Society* 48 (4): 227–242. https://doi.org/10.1080/10632921.2018.1494068.

Kuhn, T. S. 1962. *The Structure of Scientific Revolutions*. Chicago: University of Chicago Press.

Laszlo, E. 1972. *Introduction to Systems Philosophy*. New York: Gordon and Breach.

Latham, K. F., and J. Simmons. 2014. *Foundations of Museum Studies: Evolving Systems of Knowledge*. Westport, CT: Libraries Unlimited.

Lord, G. D., and N. Blankenberg. 2015. *Cities, Museums, and Soft Power*. Washington, DC: American Alliance of Museums.

Low, T. L. 1942. *The Museum as a Social Instrument*. New York: Metropolitan Museum of Art.

Macy, J. 1991. *Mutual Causality in Buddhism and General Systems Theory: The Dharma of Natural Systems*. Albany: State University of New York Press.

McGlone, P., and S. Smee 2020. "Coronavirus Shutdowns and Charges of White Supremacy: American Art Museums are in Crisis." *Washington Post*, October 12, 2020. https://www.washingtonpost.com/entertainment/museums/american-art-museums-covid-white-supremacy/2020/10/11/61094f1c-fe94-11ea-8d05-9beaaa91c71f_story.html.

Moore, K. 1994. "Introduction: Museum Management." In *Museums Management*, edited by K. Moore, 1–14. London: Routledge.

Naess, A. 1973. "The Shallow and the Deep, Long-Range Ecology Movement. A Summary." *Inquiry* 16 (1–4): 95–100. https://doi.org/10.1080/00201747308601682.

Saarinen, E., and R. Hämäläinen. 2004. "Systems Intelligence: Connecting Engineering Thinking with Human Sensitivity." In *Systems Intelligence: Discovering a Hidden Competence in Human Action and Organizational Life*, edited by E. Saarinen and R. Hämäläinen, 9–37. Helsinki: Helsinki University of Technology.

Sasaki, Y. 2017. "A Note on Systems Intelligence in Knowledge Management." *The Learning Organization* 24 (4): 236–244. https://doi.org/10.1108/TLO-09-2016-0062.

Schwab, J. J. 1960. "What Do Scientists Do?" *Behavioral Science* 5: 1–27.

Scott, W. R., and G. F. Davis. 2007. *Organizational and Organizing: Rational, Natural, and Open System Perspectives*. New York: Routledge.

Senge, P. 1990. *The Fifth Discipline*. New York: Currency Doubleday.

Senge, P., H. Hamilton, and J. Kania. 2015. "The Dawn of System Leadership." *Stanford Social Innovation Review* 13 (1): 27–33. https://ssir.org/articles/entry/the_dawn_of_system_leadership.

Shafritz, J. M., J. S. Ott, and Y. S. Jang. 2016. *Classics of Organization Theory*. 8th ed. Boston, MA: Cengage Learning.

Taylor, F. W. 1911. *The Principle of Scientific Management*. Mineola, NY: Dover Publications.

Törmänen, J., R. Hämäläinen, and E. Saarinen. 2016. "Systems Intelligence Inventory." *The Learning Organization* 23 (4): 218–231. https://doi.org/10.1108/TLO-01-2016-0006.

Von Bertalanffy, L. 1933. *Modern Theories of Development: An Introduction to Theoretical Biology*. Oxford: Oxford University Press.

Von Bertalanffy, L. 1950. "The Theory of Open Systems in Physics and Biology." *Science* 111 (2872): 23–29. https://science.sciencemag.org/content/111/2872/23.

Von Bertalanffy, L. 1972. "The History and Status of General Systems Theory." *The Academy of Management Journal* 15 (4): 23–29.

Weber, M. 1964. *The Theory of Social and Economic Organization*. New York: The Free Press.

3 Entangled realities between the museum and its community

The River Cities community

River Cities, situated across two Midwestern states and spanning six counties, is a metropolitan area including several cities and adjacent towns with a total population close to 500,000. While five large cities mostly comprise the River Cities area, there are smaller towns and cities that are also parts of it. The name River Cities, coined in the early 1900s, is not an official district title. Nonetheless, it is used ubiquitously in the area and nationwide. The region's chambers of commerce even merged creating one unifying River Cities Chamber of Commerce in the 2010s. This merging effort was to promote the greater River Cities area as one place, a way to visualize somewhat disparate cities and towns from two different states as one large interconnected metropolitan area. River Cities is a fitting metaphor to organize a community that nods to the idea of communities as networked systems.

The River Cities region encompasses five cities: Watertown and East City in the North State, and Middletown, South City, and Port City in the South State (see Figure 3.1). They have distinctive characters and have maintained their

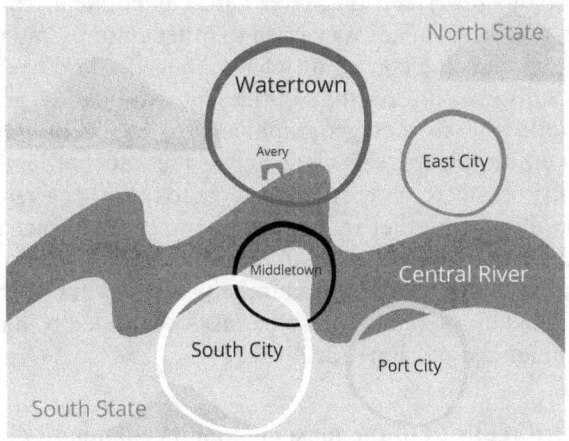

Figure 3.1 River Cities Community Joined and Divided by the Central River.

own downtowns. The Avery Art Museum is located in the largest city, Watertown. Watertown is a hub for businesses, arts and cultural organizations, and entertainment. Watertown has a casino founded in the 1990s on the waterfront of the Central River. Watertown is also home to the River Cities Chamber of Commerce, River Cities Symphony, and a baseball stadium among many other arts and cultural amenities. After the Avery moved to its current location of downtown Watertown in the beginning of the 2000s, the museum's targeted service area expanded beyond Watertown to greater River Cities. East City is mainly residential, labeled as the suburb of Watertown. Middletown, one of the most diverse communities in terms of race, ethnicity, and socioeconomic status, has welcomed a sizable number of refugees and immigrants. It is home to several arts organizations, including River Cities Ballet. South City, the second largest city in terms of population, has a sizable downtown and is home to the headquarters for several large manufacturing companies. It also has an international airport, which is used by all members of River Cities and adjacent counties. Port City is mostly suburbs to South City.

A participant described the River Cities area as follows: "it's a collection of small cities or small towns, and maybe the overall population sounds fairly big, but it feels very small" (personal communication, June 8, 2011). The entire River Cities area was small enough to get anywhere within 30 minutes with almost no traffic. However, it was large enough to have cultural and educational opportunities as well as weekly activities for community members. There were several bike paths and parks around the Central River in all cities where people could exercise and spend quality time. While education, service, and information technology industries were becoming more prominent in River Cities, manufacturing is still the top contributor to the community's economy with healthcare being the second. There is a significant farming community in the surrounding areas as well. Therefore, most study participants identified River Cities as a blue-collar community.

My participants described the River Cities as politically and culturally conservative, and as such, not very open to other cultures and perspectives. While some saw that the community had changed a lot in recent decades and had more diverse cultures than in the 1960s and 1970s, the River Cities region was noticeably divided geographically by socioeconomic status and racial and/or ethnic groups, especially across the state border. These different groups did not tend to move from one area to the other, even though they were very close to each other in terms of distance. A former development director of the museum, who grew up in the community, described this interconnected yet disconnected community by saying, "It is a community in some cases joined by a river and in some cases, separated by a river" (Lena, personal communication, June 12, 2015).

Interconnected realities of the museum and its community

The relationship between the museum and its community and surrounding areas is symbiotic. Some of these obvious interconnections between the museum and its community show how they have developed and maintained their entangled connections, thereby demonstrating how the museum has been an integral part of the community and coevolved in relation to its surroundings.

Watertown and its art gallery

The Watertown Municipal Art Gallery, the predecessor to the Avery Art Museum, was established in the 1920s. A few years previously, the state legislature approved a bill that would allow public funding to establish municipal galleries for a city with a certain population size. The intention was to establish a center serving the entire community through arts appreciation and education. A board member who had worked at the local government for decades said,

> It was the city of Watertown that went to the legislature and said, 'we would like you to allow us to use property tax to have this [art gallery],' and then the mayor gave the [art] works. We're talking about the 1920s. So, I mean, the North State really in its history has a cultural history, even though many from everywhere else just think that it's pigs and the corn and farmers.
> (Jane, personal communication, June 14, 2019)

The original location of the museum was in downtown, and then it moved to a different location away from downtown in the early 1960s. The Art Gallery was accredited by the American Alliance of Museums, then called American Association of Museums, in the 1980s and shortly after changed its name to be the Watertown Museum of Art in recognition of its newly acquired professional standing. The museum's collection, since the mayor's first donation at its establishment, has been rather organically grown through gifts and donations from local elites and philanthropists, reflecting the tastes of a few people from the community. For example, the first donor's collection mainly consisted of American, Northern European, and Central American art. Decades later, a renowned local citizen donated a substantial Caribbean art collection to the museum.

The museum's role in the revitalization of economy

The River Cities' economy boomed in the 1940s and 1950s due to its agriculture and manufacturing industries but deteriorated in the 1970s and 1980s with the farm crisis and manufacturing facilities moving out of town. The 1990s marked an urban renewal campaign with a plan to renovate abandoned buildings and hotels to create more residential spaces and to revitalize the arts scene by remodeling existing arts amenities and bringing new facilities to the downtown area. The city of Watertown viewed the brand new art museum building downtown as an anchor of this urban renewal project to bring back the economy of the city and its downtown. The North State, where the Avery is located, partly funded this revitalization plan with a grant program, which provided financial support for cultural and educational endeavors in its cities. This state grant required matching private funding from the applicant city's local community. Watertown's initial revitalization plan package was estimated to be $130 million, $20 million of which was funded with public monies including funding from the North State and the city of Watertown. The museum itself was budgeted to be $30 million, although it ended up to be more than $45 million. The construction of the new building began in early 2000s, and it opened its doors to the public in its newest and current location in the mid-2000s.

The chamber of commerce of Watertown, which was formed in the 1970s and later was merged to become the River Cities Chamber of Commerce, has been an integral part of revitalization and bringing the Avery to downtown. Chris, the director of downtown development at the River Cities Chamber of Commerce, said the plan really started with cultural amenities leading to subsequent plans for residential buildings and new commercial projects. He said,

> You know, we built this renovation of downtown on the back of the arts and that was the first thing we did to build the Music Center [music education and performance center] and the Avery....And we ended up redoing the River Cities Theater.
> (Chris, personal communication, June 13, 2019)

These initial efforts were followed by more historical building renovation projects as well as remodeling previously unoccupied buildings into residential lofts and apartments. More retail stores, bars, and restaurants followed, having more private monies invested in the downtown area, which had not been done over 30 years in Watertown. As a result, in 2019, there were over 1,500 apartments downtown compared to a few hundred at most 15 years prior. Due to these efforts, the town's economy was booming again. The GDP growth rate of the River Cities region was reported at 4% as of 2020 compared to 2.9% GDP growth rate of the entire country (pre-COVID-19). Additionally, River Cities had an unemployment rate of around 4% as of March 2020 compared to the national rate of 4.4% before COVID-19 (citation omitted for anonymity).

As an outsider to the community who visited it in 2011, 2015, and 2019, I noticed this change right away. For example, in summer 2011, the streets of downtown were empty, and I rarely saw any pedestrians. There were very few restaurants and no shopping areas that would attract people to downtown. When I came back in 2015, there were a lot more restaurants and people. Boutique shopping stores and coffee shops had popped up. I thought the change was even more dramatic in 2019; people had returned and lived in downtown, walked around, and dined at new and diverse restaurants. There was a night scene with more hotels and bars.

Moreover, by the middle of the 2010s, the River Cities region reportedly had about 100 nonprofit arts and cultural organizations according to a study conducted by Americans for the Arts with an estimated economic impact of over $70 million and about 2,000 full-time jobs in the arts (citation omitted for anonymity). This same report also indicated that people in the region travel to different parts of the community to experience the arts and spend money as a consequence—for example, going out to eat, staying at hotels, and paying for childcare—further stimulating the region's economy. The mayor of Watertown in 2019 said, it is firmly believed that the Avery is "the continual catalyst for the development of downtown" (George, personal communication, June 20, 2019).

Public and private partnership of funding arts and cultural organizations

The funding of arts organizations in River Cities and especially of the Avery was not typical in the United States. Most US arts and cultural organizations are private nonprofits, and they fund themselves through fundraising, mostly from private donors, and program service revenues. Although they receive tax benefits through federal and state income tax exemptions, they almost never receive direct governmental subsidies and grants for operating budgets. Both direct funding and operating budget grants for arts organizations were relatively common in River Cities, especially for those that were deemed to be essential arts and cultural amenities.

When the municipal art museum became a private nonprofit, the city of Watertown agreed to provide an annual operating funding of about $65,000, which was roughly a third of the museum's operating budget. The rationale behind this agreement was that the museum still stored, cared for, and exhibited the city's collection. This initial operating support, through a direct government subsidy, came with a time limit; it was supposed to either end or be reassessed by the year 2024. This new arrangement also changed the staffing structure of the museum. The museum had been staffed by the city, but from that point forward staff were no longer city employees. As this co-funding arrangement had a time limit, the museum was trying to secure further government funding beyond 2024 especially during the second time I visited the museum in 2015. Eventually the museum succeeded in securing more funding, for a longer time frame, involving other arts and cultural organizations through truly collaborative efforts. I will further discuss the result of this negotiation and the new funding structure in Chapter 5.

Another way for the community to co-fund its arts and culture is through the Arts Fund, a private nonprofit united funding agency. This organization supports the Avery for its operating budget and five other major arts and cultural organizations in River Cities. The organization was founded at the end of 2000s with the sole mission of helping the arts and cultural organizations pay for deficits so they can focus on their mission instead of making up the deficit, taking on debt, or cutting mission-critical activities. This is an alternative to a recent trend in nonprofit "businesses" as they have been taking on more auxiliary projects or functions to make themselves financially viable in carrying out their core missions (Bell 2012). The funding strategy adopted by the Arts Fund is a way to overcome the challenging tasks of meeting so many budget constraints of most nonprofits, helping important and large cultural institutions to be solvent while they focus on their mission of educating the community.

A unique advantage of this funding model is that it leverages the interconnected realities of the community and distributes funds in a way that would not be possible if left alone to each individual organization. For example, the community does not have a large population of arts and cultural donors, often having donors and board members overlapping among many cultural organizations. By raising money from wealthy people and corporations once and soliciting more public support for the arts (e.g., lobbying for both the Avery and the Science Museum in asking for new or continued city funding), it can achieve a more equitable, sustainable distribution of funds. The former CEO of the Arts Fund (Lisa, personal communication, July 15, 2015) said, "It's the organization's ability to win the hearts and minds of the people. And that's something that we as the Fund cannot do. We may be able to influence large private donors and corporations and even maybe public governments." In 2018 alone, the Arts Fund gave about $1 million to six nonprofit arts and cultural organizations that it primarily supported. Like any other funding models, however, this funding model has a downside. The most obvious one is that large and prominent arts and cultural organizations get funding over smaller ones that are more in need of support.

Filling the gap in public school arts education

The Avery fulfills an important role in arts education in public schools. Some public school teachers whom I interviewed stated that the public school education in River Cities was not balanced because it focused only on subjects that were tested and compared among states and nationwide. The superintendent of the Watertown School District echoed this sentiment stating, "Part of the problem with the schools is we're so focused on reading, writing, and arithmetic because we have to for our state national standard" (personal communication, July 7, 2015). Despite this challenge, he said his school district valued the arts because they kept students interested in school and stayed engaged in other subjects. As far as arts education goes, "we have probably the best art education in the entire region" (personal communication, July 7, 2015).

However, this has not been the case in the South State where in recent years it had state-level financial issues that resulted in cutting arts education. For example, some of the elementary school districts in the south of River Cities did not offer any visual art classes, and when they did, it was very limited. A participant said, "My son is in the South City School District and it's cut. I mean I think he is seeing art once a week now. I mean I know we're sharing a teacher that goes to four different elementary schools" (Josh, personal communication, July 2, 2015). Because of the South State's economic situation, the Avery was doing more outreach for schools in the South State than the North.

Some participants linked the lack of valuing the arts in public schools to the area's economic priorities, focusing on farming and heavy manufacturing. Although this could be an amplifying factor for this specific region's arts education, the education system in the United States lacks arts education and puts less emphasis on it. As I have argued elsewhere (Jung 2018), this is something to do with the arts being common goods as opposed to other subjects (math and science) being public goods that are deemed to be essential for the public and relevant to all people. The arts as common goods represent intangible and noneconomic values (Helfrich 2012; Lohmann 1989) and may not be relevant to all people depending on individual values and preferences (Jung 2018). Echoing this view, arts have been considered something that is extra and that does not need to be taught to all people (Day 1998). This is not going to change anytime soon so the educational role of the Avery and other nonprofit arts and cultural institutions is critical.

The Avery was one of the several informal (non-mandatory) educational sites that try to fill the arts education gap in the public educational infrastructure of River Cities. For example, the River Cities Symphony and the Music Center emphasize music education while the Avery and other visual arts organizations focused on visual art education through their exhibitions, programs, and hands-on art-making classes and workshops. Specifically for the Avery, Education was the largest department of the museum and did a substantial amount of outreach (reaching over 30,000 students annually by 2018), playing an essential role of providing arts education to the region's kindergarten through 12th grade (K-12) students.

Collaboration among arts and cultural organizations

As mentioned earlier, River Cities is home to over 100 nonprofit arts and cultural organizations. Three of the larger and more established arts and cultural organizations include the Science Museum (Watertown, 1870s), the River Cities Symphony (Watertown, 1900s), and the River Cities Theater (Watertown, 1930s). Younger and more recent arts and cultural institutions include the Central Zoo (Middletown, 1960s), the River Cities Arts Organization (Middletown, 1970s), the River Cities Ballet (Middletown, 1990s), the Botanical Garden (Middletown, 1990s), the Children's Museum (East City, 1990s), and the Music Center (Watertown, 2000s).

The Avery maintained partnerships with some arts, cultural, and educational organizations in the area. For example, the museum was trying to establish partnerships with other arts organizations such as the River Cities

Symphony and the River Cities Ballet. During my visit in 2011, the museum's former associate curator and other staff members had met with representatives from the Symphony and Ballet groups to discuss possible partnerships and collaboration in programming and event planning based on themes of museum exhibitions. Since then, these partnerships have exploded. By the time I visited the museum the third time in 2019, these organizations had just completed a community-wide arts and cultural project that revolved around the Avery's exhibition on European masters. During three months, more than 40 organizations held contemporaneous exhibitions, programs, and events that were all related to the theme of the exhibition. For example, the Science Museum showed a movie about one of the European masters featured at the Avery exhibition, and the Symphony opened its season with a masterwork concert and ended it with a chamber concert at the Avery. This truly showed how much the museum has grown to be a leader and productive partner among arts and cultural organizations in the region. An education staff said,

> The museum is much more interwoven in the fabric of the community. I think the community relies on us to be sort of the leader in the arts and cultural entertainment....connecting with places like the symphony, the Music Center, the ballet. We do stuff together.
> (Holly, personal communication, June 7, 2019)

Disconnected realities of the museum and its community

While the museum is necessarily interconnected with its community as described above, some relationships and realities between the two were disconnected creating further challenges for the museum to become more inclusive and relevant. As discussed in Chapter 2, museums have traditionally served a certain group of population that tend to be white, affluent, and well educated (Farrell and Medvedeva 2010). Therefore, museums have maintained a narrow connection to its community not serving its wider community. The Avery is not an exception to this. This section discusses the areas of the museum and community relationship that are disconnected or misaligned.

Elitist perception of the Avery in the community

While the museum has been an important part of the region, most people in the community had certain perceptions about the Avery. Many participants mentioned that the Avery is perceived as an elitist institution. A community nonprofit director observed, "It's not an active place....it's an exclusive art club....Don't present yourself as a museum of the community if you're not serving the community" (Josh, personal communication, July 2, 2015). Generally speaking, the elitist perception is one of the largest challenges that many art museums face in the United States and even worldwide. Even though the Avery changed its mission from traditional and collection-focused to a more education-oriented approach when it moved to a new location, many community members still expressed that the museum did not fully belong to the community.

While there could be many elements that contributed to this elitist notion of the Avery, I discuss the two most cited reasons based on interviews with the participants: the name of the museum and public funding of a private art museum. First, the name Avery is often associated with the private wealth and the banking business of the Avery family. The former director of the River Cities Chamber of Commerce and former board member said, "It [the Avery] still carries the legacy of being very much a club of the highbrow, of the art-loving elite of our community" (personal communication, July 11, 2011). She continued, "It carries the unintended burden of the single biggest investor [donor] of the Avery family and having the building named after it" (personal communication, July 11, 2011). Especially during my first visit in 2011, many community members, mistakenly, considered the museum as a private asset of the Avery family, and, therefore, had less sense of ownership when compared with other arts and cultural institutions.

Additionally, its developmental history of getting public money to build and continuously fund a private nonprofit museum was seen by some as a "waste of public money" when the streets needed repairs and sewage systems replaced. Former mayor of Watertown said, "The city's total budget is about $220 million and fixing the streets is about $800 million. Art is not a priority compared to this" (Douglas, personal communication, July 15, 2015). A local small business owner (2015), who has lived in the community for over a decade and had never visited the museum, shared this sentiment stating that people are negative toward the Avery and worried about tax money going to the museum. The mayor in 2015 expressed that supporting the museum with tax dollars is not fair because the museum was often used by a handful of people who tended to be wealthier, whiter, and better educated. While this argument suggested that tax monies that were collected by all people should not fund something that is used by only a few, public funding of the museum was one of the very reasons that makes the museum integral part of its city. Public funding of the museum could send a message that art museums are important, although they must be worthy of wider support.

Intimidating look of the museum building

At the inception, the board of directors invited many architects from all over the world to submit design ideas, and they eventually chose a world-famous architect and his firm from overseas to design the museum's new building. The architect's vision was to design a building that could be a major catalyst for urban revitalization of Watertown. His intention was to attract diverse people to the downtown area with the new building while maintaining the traditional outline of the old city. The completed building looks very different from the surrounding scenery. It is a simple volumetric block enveloped by translucent glass surfaces. A former director described the museum as "a resident museum in a tourist museum building" (Ken, personal communication, July 3, 2015). The context and environment matter because if the museum were to be somewhere else, it would send a different message. A visiting artist who came to the Avery for the first time remarked, "This is an amazing building. Are you kidding? If this building was anywhere else, it would be a world-class institution" (personal communication, June 13, 2015).

Many participants shared that the museum building was not well thought out at the inception. Before the building was constructed, the committee, who was charged with the new building plan, worked with a group of consultants to conduct a feasibility study that tried to assess the appropriate size of the museum for anticipated number of visitors and users as well as other financial implications. A board member blamed the accuracy of the feasibility study for the disproportionately larger museum size (it was $15 million over the initial budget) compared to the small number of visitors. A former board member who was involved in the museum's new building project said,

> We wanted something that could be an icon that really took this community to a different level...wasn't just a same old stage kind of process and that's why we got criticized a little bit about not using a local architect.
> (Margaret, personal communication, June 30, 2015)

She argued that it was the right decision to build a bigger museum that the community could grow into.

Exterior of the building

The Avery's building looks like a minimalist artwork. When I first visited the museum in 2011, it looked like a new house where occupants had not quite moved in yet. A museum staff member described the building: an "alien spaceship has landed here" (Eric, personal communication, June 23, 2015). There were mixed feelings toward the aesthetic qualities of the building. Some loved it, while others expressed their dislikes. However, with time, the museum became the symbol of Watertown and even of the greater River Cities region. Some people referred to it as the "jewel box" of the community, provoking the feeling of excellence designed by a world-renowned architect.

Unlike the mixed feelings toward the building itself, most people unanimously disliked the museum's large plaza in front of the main entrance. It is composed of a parking lot on one side, and two benches, small trees, and a minimalist looking geometric sculpture on the other side. This plaza makes the Avery building recessed from the street approximately 200 feet, creating a visual and physical distance from the street, making it look formidable and out of reach. A local artist described it as "that imposing walk of death up to the Avery" (Roy, personal communication, June 25, 2015). A board member said, "you are crossing a wasteland to get to the front door" (Patricia, personal communication, June 16, 2015). The plaza has not changed much when I went back to the museum the second and third times.

Interior of the building

Upon entering, the visitors first saw the lobby area which was quite large at almost 4,000 square feet. The lobby floor was covered with large shiny black tiles. A large black desk covered almost the entire length of the wall facing the Central River when I first visited in 2011. No one sat at the desk to greet visitors except on weekends or during events. There was a psychological hesitation when people walked into the museum, which was captured in this notion of threshold fear that constrains people from fully participating in activities or entering a space that is meant for them (Gurian 2005). A director of a local historical center put it this way: "Maybe the building itself is a barrier for some people…I think there's certain self-consciousness that occurs right at that step-in moment like 'Should we even be doing this?'" (personal communication, July 9, 2015). While the lobby area served as a significant source of rental revenue for the museum, generating even more than admission fees, a number of participants criticized the lobby space for being too intimidating. The galleries were clean and sterile and had a very high ceiling and most of the walls were white. This was very much in line with the white-cube approach that displays artwork in order to provide only the "necessary conditions for proper (visual, non-political) consumption of serious painting" (McClellan 2003, 25).

Participants mentioned how the building was not up to the Americans with Disabilities Act (ADA) standards in some areas. For example, there was a mezzanine level that was facing the Central River. While it was a lovely space to enjoy the scenery and take a break, it was only accessible through one set of stairs. Additionally, most doors in the gallery did not have an automatic door opener installed. Some of these were easier to fix than others but were expensive to retrofit nonetheless. According to a local artist who worked closely with the museum, the architect made a mistake overlooking some of these ADA requirements. He said, "This building was designed after 1993 when they had ADA. So it's not like this is some old thing that had to be retrofitted. He just didn't care" (Zach, personal communication, June 12, 2019). According to visitor survey results in 2019, some visitors commented about the lack of a family restroom for a disabled family member, the lack of seating during events and talks, and no measures taken for visually impaired attendees. Unlike the plaza, there were changes made to the interior of the museum, such as getting rid of the big black desk and making the entrance more inviting with actual human faces greeting visitors. However, the ADA requirements had not been updated at the time of 2019.

Fear of art: lack of cultural capital

The community's perception of elitism and their threshold fear toward the museum are related to the age-old idea that arts are not for everyone. Many people "fear" visual art and art museums, and as a result they do not use or support them. Several participants said that community members are intimidated to walk into an art museum because they think they do not understand art. A local artist and retired professor, Roy, said, "Most people in the community feel that they are an idiot in an art museum so they just don't go" (personal communication, July 13, 2011). Some non-visitors I interviewed stated that visiting the museum is just not their thing or their priority. For example, a local resident who lived in the community for about 20 years shared that she has never been to the Avery. When I asked why, she responded that it is not something she does and has no spare time for "something like that" (personal communication, June 10, 2015). A local artist pointed out that the community is largely blue collar and a lot of people do not associate with the museum-going culture because they think it is for only "smart" people. "As long as you bread it, fry it, and serve it with ranch dressing we'll eat it. They're really timid about things" (Zach, personal communication, June 12, 2019).

Bourdieu's concept of cultural capital can explain why some people may not visit museums. Cultural capital is something that can be inherited from family members at the earliest days of life (Bourdieu 1984). For example, a person who was exposed to more educational opportunities and museum culture as a child tends to have the knowledge and language to talk about arts and culture in museum settings. When people lack cultural capital of specialized knowledge of art history and visual culture and a cultivated aesthetic taste, it becomes difficult for them to understand or appreciate museum experiences, especially in art museums that are perceived as an elite culture often associated with the middle and upper-middle classes (Bourdieu 1984; Schwarzer 2006). When people are not confident going into an art museum or exploring visual art experiences due to their lack of cultural capital, they do not visit museums and as a result they will not bring their children to the museum either, which creates a cycle of not valuing museum-going.

A docent explained that when she led a tour, some people were terrified to say things or answer her questions because they were afraid of saying something wrong or stupid. In other words, they did not possess the type of cultural capital habitually used in the museum field. Some visitors said in an interview that they feared things that they were not familiar with. I observed one visitor who looked very uncomfortable looking at paintings, and shortly after I interviewed her. She said that she felt like she did not belong here at the museum and did not know what to do in galleries. This first time visitor said, "I grew up in a very, very small town. The closest one [art museum] is probably about two hours away. I don't paint and draw and, you know, I'm not an artist at all" (personal communication, August 2, 2011). Another local resident who sometimes visited the Avery said, "It's [the Avery] not important [to me] and more for the elite or a certain population" (personal communication, June 16, 2015). She emphasized she valued the arts but felt uncomfortable trying to enjoy the arts at the Avery.

Demographics of the community, board and staff, and visitors

Many participants said River Cities is diverse for the Midwest in terms of race, ethnicity, and culture, but they also emphasized that the Midwest as a whole is not very diverse except some areas. The North State is a lot more homogeneous compared to the South State. The overall racial breakdown of the North State is 85% white (not Hispanic or Latino), 4% black, 6% Hispanic, and 3% Asian, and the South State is composed of 61% white (not Hispanic or Latino), 15% black, 18% Hispanic or Latino, and 6% Asian. River Cities' population spanning between these two different states tracks this trend well, having the north side of River Cities being more homogenous than the south side. For example, Watertown, located in the North State, is made up of 75% white (not Hispanic or Latino), 11% black, 9% Hispanic or Latino, 3% Asian, and 3% two or more races. In the South State, Middletown consists of 62% white (not Hispanic or Latino), 20% black, 11% Hispanic or Latino, 4% Asian, and 4% two or more races (citation omitted for anonymity).

These two sub-communities separated by the river are also distinctive in terms of educational level and income. While about 20% of the population of River Cities and surrounding areas has a bachelor's degree or higher, there is a stark difference between communities in the North and South States. The North State side of River Cities has 33% of the population with a bachelor's degree or higher, while the South State side has 24% for the same category. In 2020, the median household income was over $70,000 for the North State and was a little over $53,000 for the South State. Additionally, many persons of poverty live in Middletown, reporting more than 20% living below poverty level (citation omitted for anonymity). A director of a nonprofit that provides after-school education opportunities in Middletown said, "78% of the students enrolled at our schools are recipients of free or reduced lunch, this tells where they sit socioeconomically" (Josh, personal communication, July 2, 2015). These diverse characteristics and demographics of community members were not reflected in board, staff, and visitor demographics, which are discussed below.

Board and staff demographics

The same group of people tended to support all nonprofit arts and cultural organizations in River Cities, creating a risk to sustainability of nonprofit arts governance and support. Some claimed it was difficult to find new board members because the same people who are interested in the arts were on several different boards already. Unfortunately, these arts supporters and volunteer board members were homogeneous: white, older, wealthy, and better educated not reflecting the wider River Cities' population. The staff members were also predominantly white and highly educated. From 2011 to 2019, the museum only maintained one person of color on staff who was the office administrator for the museum out of 21 staff members (e.g., the museum had 17 full-time staff members and 4 part-time members in 2019). Some people of color occupied security and restaurant staff but were not direct employees of the museum because these functions were outsourced from other companies.

Unfortunately, this is very typical of museum leadership and staff composition. Many scholars have noted the tendency of museum staff to be homogeneous culturally, socioeconomically, and educationally (Farrell and Medvedeva 2010; Fleming 2002; McClellan 2003). Trustees and senior-level museum professionals are predominantly white, upper-middle class, and well educated (Farrell and Medvedeva 2010). Forty-six percent of museum boards are all white, not including any one person of color (AAM 2018). While there are an increasing number of female directors and more diversity in staff composition across most ranks, most senior leadership positions are still held by white males (Westermann, Schonfeld, and Sweeney 2019). The proportion of white senior officers in major US art museums is higher than in other corporations, universities, and government offices (Lufkin 2009).

Snapshot of visitor demographics

Not reflecting the community's overall demographics, participants have said that the Avery's visitors and patrons were white, older, and well educated, repeatedly the same people coming to events and programs. Others including board members echoed this sentiment saying that the Avery visitors were not representative of the community, and my visitor survey results fully supported this, which is discussed in Chapter 5. Some participants pointed out that this was because the museum did not really reach out to some sub-communities that are more diverse than the museum's immediate surrounding areas. In other words, the North State, where the museum is located, is more homogeneous than the South State, and the residents of the North State are the primary users of the museum. The perception is that the Avery did not provide services to a broader community. Some board members and staff seemed frustrated by the fact that the museum was not reaching the wider community even though they were trying to get people from the South State and other rural areas to visit the museum. The discussion of staff and board diversity is further covered in Chapter 4, while I will cover visitor diversity in greater detail in Chapter 5.

Discussion

One of the most important characteristics of an open system is that it is open to its environment influencing and being influenced by it. The Avery is an open system and has interacted with its surroundings over time. The city government from the outset was crucial in establishing the predecessor of the museum and has been funding the newly established Avery even though it was no longer a city museum. The renewed museum was fundamental in the region's economic development plan and in revitalizing downtown Watertown. The museum was not only supported by various individuals from the community but also from a local united arts funding agency, Arts Fund, receiving a substantial portion of its operating budget through this community organization. Due to the lack of arts education in K-12 education of River Cities, the museum played an important role in filling the visual art education gap. Lastly, it collaborated with multiple arts and cultural organizations to provide more educational, artistic, and social opportunities to its community. These interconnected accounts demonstrate that the museum is necessarily part of its community. The community affects the museum by providing inputs of resources and partnerships, and the museum in turn influences the various elements of its larger environment, such as the local government, education system, and other arts and cultural organizations. These elements all together form an interconnected web of organizations and social structure in River Cities.

However, there were many accounts that demonstrated the museum's disconnection from its community. The museum was seen by many as an elitist institution because of the new name of the museum and how some community members saw public funding of the private museum problematic. The intimidating look of the building inside and out and lack of accommodation for individuals with disabilities were factors contributing to how the museum seemed out of place and not a comfortable space for everyone. The community had a history of not valuing the arts and lacked the type of cultural capital that traditional art museums require their visitors to possess. Related to all these aforementioned factors, only a small portion of the community used the museum. There was certainly a correlation between who worked at the museum and who visited it, creating a gap between the museum and its larger community. The most visible issue was the lack of diverse race and ethnicity in museum leadership, staff, and visitors. However, the less visible lack of diversity of socioeconomic status and education was at play as well because the less wealthy or less educated did not seem to visit the museum. While it is a field-wide issue, this type of disconnection and the practice that reinforces it are contradictory to most museums' obligation to serve the diverse publics due to their legal structure as nonprofits. They receive certain tax benefits in exchange for fulfilling their educational mission as per the IRS to serve all people, not just a certain group of people (Jung 2015).

Inseparable connection

Although the museum was disconnected to certain aspects of its community, it is never a separate entity from its surroundings. Disconnected realities, when continued without meaningful intervention, can hurt the museum and community even more in the long term. For example, when the museum's leaders, staff, and visitors are not aligned with the community at large, it risks becoming an organization that is out of touch from the rest of the community, used only by a handful of people who tend to be privileged in many ways. If diverse publics do not see the point of funding museums because they do not use them, museums could lose public funding and perhaps their rationale for existence as nonprofit organizations that receive tax exemptions and other private supports. The Avery has been intimately related to people who hold power, wealth, and influence. For instance, philanthropists donated artworks and local elites helped fund the new building. This involvement of people in power shaped the museum's nature and content, reflecting their tastes and values, telling their stories, and interpreting the arts of others from their perspectives not through more inclusive and source community (i.e., owners of the material heritage, arts, and culture displayed at museums) oriented lenses. Museums have excluded a certain group of people "not by accident but by design" (Fleming 2002, 213). The values and tastes of an elitist minority, who has historically established and run museums, have affected what museums have collected, how they have been managed, and for whom they have tailored their programs, restricting themselves to meeting the needs and interests of a few powerful groups (Fleming, 2002).

Lack of community input for the Avery

In some ways, taking on a new identity as the Avery created more challenges to the museum to be inclusive and diverse with its new location, building, name, and mission. The new Avery museum project may have been seen as a passion project of a few, who planned and executed the project with their assumptions not consulted with the community members most affected by it (e.g., potential users and funders through their property tax). While the Avery's building ended up to be an amazing facility stimulating the community's economy tremendously and accommodating more people in recent years, the museum project did not reflect the wider community's input. Maybe this is why the visitor composition had not changed although the museum diversified its programs and exhibitions and was getting more total number of visitors (further discussed in Chapter 5). According to my participants, there were committees, feasibility studies, and focus groups, but there was not an effort to collect the community input widely. For example, the input may have been collected from board members of the museum. However, no one mentioned if a resident of Watertown, who lived down the road from the museum and whose property tax supported the museum project, wanted it or not. The burden of the museum built based on the assumption of what the community needed but not asking its actual needs was still felt in the museum's overall practice and visitorship. The process may have isolated many people who still thought that the museum was a waste of public money and did not feel they belonged to the museum.

Recognizing the gap as an opportunity for change

The elitist perception toward the museum and the disconnection between the museum and its wider community were not mere perceptions but an impression that had been ingrained in people's mind over time based on their interaction with and knowledge about the museum. "Every museum exhibition, whatever its overt subject, inevitably draws on the cultural assumptions and resources of the people who make it" (Lavine and Karp 1991, 1). In other words, the mental models of important players of the museum are necessarily reflected in the museum's output that speaks directly to a narrow group of people who already support it. This is a negative feedback loop that reinforces the existing mental models and does not lead to transformational changes. Yet, this can create a perfect condition for the museum to trigger a positive feedback function to change. When there is a mismatch between the museum visitors and the overall population of the community, the museum can gather more input from those who do not visit the museum and try to transform its mental models, structure, and culture (i.e., throughputs) that their programs and exhibitions are based on, which can generate new outputs that would match the wider audience needs, not just those of the traditional narrow group.

References

AAM (American Alliance of Museums). 2018. *Facing Change: Insights from the American Alliance of Museums' Diversity, Equity, Accessibility, and Inclusion Working Group*. Arlington, VA: American Alliance of Museums. https://www.aam-us.org/wp-content/uploads/2018/04/AAM-DEAI-Working-Group-Full-Report-2018.pdf.

Bell, F. 2012. "How are Museums Supported Financially in the U.S.?" *United States Department of State, Bureau of International Information Programs*. https://photos.state.gov/libraries/amgov/133183/english/P_You_Asked_How_Are_Museums_Supported_Financially.pdf.

Bourdieu, P. 1984. *Distinction: A Social Critique of the Judgment of Taste*. Cambridge, MA: Harvard University Press.

Day, M. D. 1998. "Art Education: Essential for a Balanced Education." *NASSP Bulletin* 82 (597): 1–7. https://doi.org/10.1177/019263659808259702.

Farrell, B., and M. Medvedeva. 2010. *Demographic Transformation and the Future of Museums*. Washington, DC: American Association of Museums.

Fleming, D. 2002. "Positioning the Museum for Social Inclusion." In *Museums, Society, Inequality*, edited by R. Sandell, 213–224. New York: Routledge.

Gurian, E. H. 2005. "Threshold Fear." In *Reshaping Museum Space: Architecture, Design, Exhibitions,* edited by S. MacLeod, 203–214. London: Routledge.

Helfrich, S. 2012. "Common Goods Don't Simply Exist–They Are Created." In *The Wealth of the Commons: A World beyond Market and State,* edited by D. Bollier and S. Helfrich, 61–67. Amherst, MA: Levellers Press.

Jung, Y. 2015. "Diversity Matters: Theoretical Understanding of and Suggestions for the Current Fundraising Practices of Nonprofit Art Museums." *The Journal of Arts Management, Law, and Society* 45 (4): 255–268. https://doi.org/10.1080/10632921.2015.1103672.

Jung, Y. 2018. "Economic Discussion of Conflict between Public Education Policies and Common Good Arts in the United States." *The Journal of Arts Management, Law, and Society* 48 (2): 98–107. https://doi.org/10.1080/10632921.2017.1303412.

Lavine, S. D., and I. Karp. 1991. "Introduction: Museums and Multiculturalism." In *Exhibition Cultures: The Poetics and Politics of Museum Display,* edited by I. Karp and S. D. Lavine, 1–9. Washington, DC: Smithsonian Institution.

Lohmann, R. A. 1989. "And Lettuce Is Nonanimal: Toward a Positive Economics of Voluntary Action." *Nonprofit and Voluntary Sector Quarterly* 18 (4): 367–383. https://doi.org/10.1177/089976408901800407.

Lufkin, M. 2009. "America Is Changing—But Are Its Art Museums?" *Art Newspaper,* June 30, 2009. https://www.theartnewspaper.com/archive/america-is-changing-but-are-its-art-museums.

McClellan, A. 2003. "A Brief History of Art Museum Public." In *Art and Its Publics: Museum Studies at the Millennium,* edited by A. McClellan, 1–50. Oxford: Blackwell Publishing.

Schwarzer, M. 2006. *Riches, Rivals, and Radicals: 100 Years of Museum in America.* Washington, DC: American Association of Museums.

Westermann, M., R. Schonfeld, and L. Sweeney. 2019. *Art Museum Staff Demographic Survey 2018.* Andrew W. Mellon Foundation. https://mellon.org/media/filer_public/b1/21/b1211ce7-5478-4a06-92df-3c88fa472446/sr-mellon-report-art-museum-staff-demographic-survey-01282019.pdf.

4 Museum throughputs and mental models

Museum open system and its throughput constructs

Chapter 3 demonstrates how the museum was part of its larger community, and how the museum and its community affected each other. Here, the focus shifts to the internal open system of the museum, which I describe as throughputs of the museum. In other words, the museum as a social system received inputs (e.g., information, money, and human resources) from the external community and created outputs (e.g., programs and exhibitions) to the community. People the museum attracted and their feedback became the result of the outputs, which were fed back to the museum system as inputs. So the cycle continued. In other words, throughputs are the internal systems of a museum that make the transformation from inputs to outputs possible, creating the mutual causality loop between the museum and its environment. More specifically, I will discuss the structure and culture of the museum as major throughput components of the museum open system and examine mental models behind these throughput components.

Structure

The museum's recent organizational chart, which is anonymized and slightly modified in Figure 4.1, shows the surface structure of the museum, including staff and departmental organization. The Avery followed a traditional, typical museum hierarchical structure. I saw three versions of the organizational chart from the museum in 2011, 2015, and 2019, and the basic structure stayed almost the same with no substantial changes. As a governing body, the museum had 22 board members, with seven of them constituting an executive committee along with the chief executive officer (CEO). The board worked with the CEO (the terms director and executive director are also used interchangeably with CEO) to set and reinforce policies, create strategic plans, and make executive decisions. The CEO served as a liaison between the board and the staff. The head of each department reported to the CEO and occasionally worked with board and committee members. The Security Department and Catering Services (i.e., restaurant services)

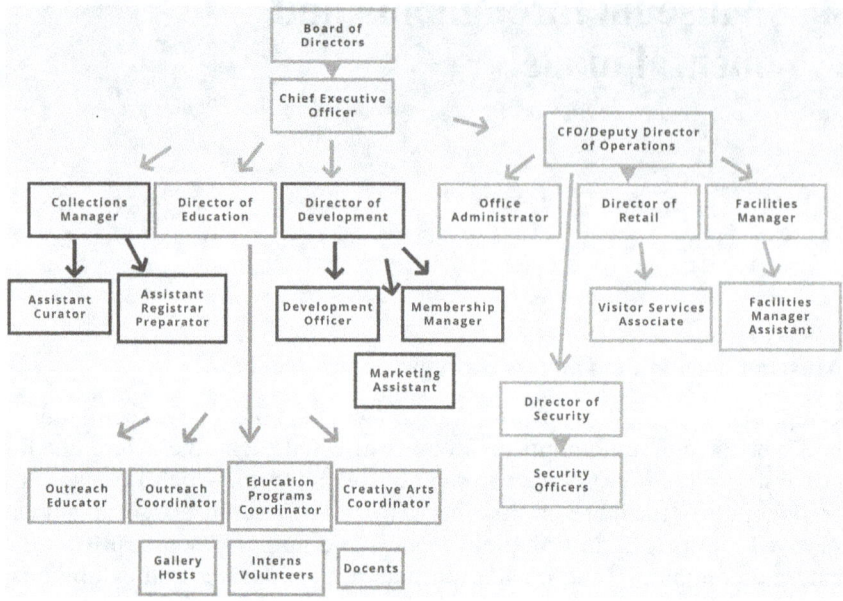

Figure 4.1 Avery Art Museum Organizational Chart.

were contracted, and ultimately reported to the CEO through the chief financial officer (CFO) who also assumed the role of the deputy director of operations. In 2011, the CFO, Ed, fulfilled the role of acting CEO to fill the gap in between directors. The museum hired its immediate former CEO in 2012, Joe, and he stayed at the museum for seven years before he resigned in the summer of 2019. The museum was able to hire a new executive director replacing Joe at the end of 2019. Since she was hired after I completed my data collection for this book, I did not interview her.

The board

A board of directors at a nonprofit is the fiduciary body officially and legally in charge of the organization (National Council of Nonprofits n.d.). The Avery's board consisted of local executives, entrepreneurs, and leaders who were economically comfortable and well established in the community. Board members came from different geographic sections of River Cities and brought various expertise to the Avery. About three quarters of them resided in the North State, which is less diverse and more affluent compared to the South State. Overall, in terms of their race, ethnicity, age, and socioeconomic backgrounds, its board members were not representative of the community. In 2015, from 22 board members, the board included only one person of color, and no relatively young people (under 40 years old). In 2019, there were two new members of color and at least one younger member (under 40 years old) on the board. One former board member (2015) recalling his 25-year history with the museum said he remembered only two black board members. While board members' roles and degrees of participation differed, most of whom I interviewed agreed that their primary roles were fundraising, policy-making, managing funds, managing the CEO, and encouraging the community at large to be interested in the museum. One area of board responsibility that was highly emphasized was the fundraising capacity of the board. For example, the board as a whole was *recommended* to raise $200,000 a year.

Each board term was three years but it could be extended without a break up to nine years. Board members who served the maximum nine years could come back on the board after a year break. The Avery's term model could potentially have board members for decades with only short breaks. BoardSource, a nonprofit that provides support and resources for nonprofit governance and leadership, emphasizes that having a healthy term limit is important to make it easier to diversify a board and to avoid "the perpetual concentration of power within a small group of people and the intimidation of new members by this dominant group" (BoardSource 2019). The Avery maintained a core group of board members since the beginning of operation at the new location or even before. A board member, who was rotating off at the time of the interview in 2019, mentioned that four of the long-term board members were leaving after nine years of service due to the term limit and they had been seriously involved with the museum. She expressed concern that the board dynamic would change while recognizing it as an opportunity to bring in new voices.

Board expertise

More than half of board members had a background in business and held or had held prominent executive positions at corporations in the region. For example, in 2011, the board president was the CEO of a local insurance company. In 2015, an executive from a local wealth management company served as the president, and in 2019, another bank executive carried on this responsibility. The board also included attorneys who could assist with the museum's legal areas of planned giving, copyright, or employment. In addition, it included members with marketing, arts, and medical backgrounds. A few members of the board had arts-related backgrounds and expertise. For example, one board member was the director of another visual arts organization in the community. Some board members were considered "art smart" because they collected art themselves. Most board members whom I interviewed stated that they enjoyed and appreciated art but were not experts of art, art history, or arts organizations. While the occupational backgrounds of members benefited the museum, one may question whether these decision-makers could fully understand the concerns and aspirations of the community as a whole.

For a board of about 22, having so few members with expertise in the museum industry or nonprofit management was unfortunate. A former museum staff member said, "I was often frustrated with board members as consultants because they're there to set policies and to apply that. However, I was bothered by the fact that they did not understand our industry most of the time" (personal communication, July 15, 2011). He questioned whether board members were in the best position to advocate for the museum when they did not have a full understanding of how an art museum functions and relates to the larger community. A senior staff member echoed this sentiment in that board members would often say, "I run a business...and why can't you do something like that?" (personal communication, June 12, 2019). As an example, the senior staff member elaborated that some board members suggested implementing commission-based compensation as incentives; "If they reach these sorts of goals, then they get 10% or something like that" (personal communication, June 12, 2019). In nonprofits, this model is not appropriate and sometimes considered unethical. For example, the Association of Fundraising Professionals (2014) prohibits its members from entering into a contract based on a percentage of contributions because this practice may lead professionals to making decisions based on their personal financial gains, not the best interests of the donors or those of the organization.

The board's lack of understanding in the nonprofit museum work is not just a problem of the Avery. Most nonprofit boards' skills in corporate business management styles and principles cannot be transferred to a museum setting because museums have different ideological, economic, and political values (Moore 1994). In addition, since most board members did not have experience managing an art museum or specific knowledge of the content area, their knowledge and management skills sometimes did not apply to a nonprofit art museum (Griffin 2008; Janes and Sandell 2019). A former director of the Avery, Ken (personal communication, 2015), said that people from the corporate world often do not understand that nonprofits have multiple bottom lines and quality is more important than making profits. As a career museum executive, he was often frustrated with many museum boards in general, not just at the Avery.

Board qualifications

While members volunteered to serve on the board and do not get compensated for it, the expected commitment to act as a legal fiduciary and their qualifications and pressure to do so were unrealistic. In this way, the legal and structural set-up of a nonprofit organization is somewhat flawed. "In no other sector do we find a group of part-time, uncompensated individuals who govern with varying levels of expertise and organizational allegiance but remain nonetheless legally in charge of an organization" (Gazley 2009, 86). Several board members pointed out that some rarely participated or did not come to the regular meetings. One board member said, "I've been on the board for almost two years and I saw one guy for the first time last time we had a meeting and I haven't missed anything" (Patricia, personal communication, June 16, 2015). According to another board member, "they give you an actual contract every year. You sign a commitment. Trying to get those contracts back [signed and returned] is crazy" (personal communication, June 30, 2015).

A non-board member of one of the museum's committees commented on the unrealistic nature of board qualifications—money, skills, and influence—suggesting an alternative model to structure board of directors looking at their commitment, knowledge, and willingness to work. The committee member said, "Does money have to be part of being a board of directors?...Their exclusivity is limiting accessibility....Maybe there is another model where board of directors don't have to give money" (personal communication, June 23, 2015). This point was echoed by a local artist and retired professor who would have liked to have been on the Avery board but could not due to his inability to give. He pointed out,

> The Avery is probably at the top of my list of things that I would like to throw some energy into. If I'd taken a different path and instead of getting a teacher's salary, which is not massive, and if I were more affluent I would try to be an effective financial contributor. Yeah I would like to be on the board. I think it's good to have somebody who's not only an artist but an academic.
> (Roy, personal communication, June 25, 2015)

Leadership

Since the Avery opened its new facility, it has experienced frequent director turnover. Prior to 2012, there had been two executive directors and three interim directors over a period of approximately six years. This trend ceased when the museum hired Joe in 2012, who stayed until 2019.

Brief history of CEOs

According to one staff member, the former director during the move to a new location was good at making the transition but was not confident enough to lead and maintain it. After she was let go, a board member filled the director role as an interim director. The former CEO, Ken, was hired in 2007 after 18 months without a director, and he managed the museum for about three and a half years until the end of 2011. The overall consensus of his directorship was that he initiated the movement toward a more proactive, inviting, and friendly posture. Before Ken officially submitted his resignation, the board of directors felt the need to bring someone in from outside the organization to lead the Avery in an attempt to minimize bias and emotion in decision-making. They recruited Deborah, who was also the director of another visual arts organization in River Cities, to be a board member before Ken left. She was subsequently asked to serve as an interim director upon Ken's departure. Deborah quickly made a number of significant decisions, including eliminating positions and reducing programming to the point of minimal operation. Deborah (personal communication, 2011) said that these changes were necessary until a solution to the budget deficit could be identified and put in place. She served as the interim director of the Avery for about eight months. When she stepped down, the CFO, Ed, served as an acting director until Joe was hired in 2012. Thus, during my first visit in 2011, Ed was the acting director, and for my second and third visits in 2015 and 2019, Joe was the CEO.

Down-to-earth leadership

Many agreed that Joe was instrumental in making the museum more accessible. Several staff members commented that he was very approachable, and this quality carried through with donors and artists. A long-time donor commented, "He hand wrote me a thank you note…and I thought this day and age of email to get it handwritten in the mail.…That kind of personal attention and detail made me…feel like he was listening to me" (personal communication, July 7, 2015). A local artist said, "Joe is really earthy and a really good communicator.…The Avery is a much more lively place, a much more happy place" (Roy, personal communication, June 25, 2015). He compared Joe to the previous director, Ken, who, in his opinion, was more academic and elitist. Although Joe had never stepped foot in the North State prior to his interview for the job, he embraced the community, tried to understand it by showing up and interacting with people, and was effective in making genuine connections with a lot of stakeholders and organizations in River Cities. An education staff member, who worked at the museum for over ten years at the time of the interview, commented,

> He is the only director who shows up at every single family day [one of the museum programs]. We joked that he is certified to teach the spinner [an art making tool] because he volunteers to do it. He's in almost every program that we do.
> (Rebecca, personal communication, June 12, 2019)

The CFO said,

> I think part of our increase in visitor traffic is because of Joe. I think he's initiated a number of things that help people feel more comfortable with a fine art museum. I think he embraced our community. I think he got out in our community, he made friends, he was accessible.
> (Ed, personal communication, June 12, 2019)

Delegative leadership

Joe's leadership style can be described as delegative leadership rather than authoritative or controlling. Noah, assistant registrar and preparator at the Avery, said Joe was different from other museum directors he has known who tend to be very extroverted and bombastic. Noah said, "He [Joe] kind of leads with a gentle hand, and I think that it was a good dynamic for this institution" (personal communication, June 14, 2019). A board member shared this view stating that Joe was a conscientious leader. "He is very aware of all the decisions he's making and he's very careful" (Margaret, personal communication, June 30, 2015).

Multiple staff members also mentioned that Joe was very good at letting staff experiment without micromanaging. The director of education, Emily, said, the director "has embraced the power of the word 'yes'….and that has allowed us to really experiment our ways that have naturally gotten us to where we are" (personal communication, June 10, 2019). The museum's assistant curator, Olivia, also said,

> I worked with him on a couple of exhibitions, and there's a lot of back and forth. And even when I was an intern, he wanted to hear my opinions.…It wasn't just something where he was throwing me things to do.
> (Personal communication, June 10, 2019)

Some staff members found the CEO to be too passive and not actively managing staff, even becoming too laissez-faire from time to time. This could be a byproduct of his leadership style of being delegative. Some staff emphasized that the director needed to be more assertive and make firm and harsh decisions that certain behaviors were not tolerated, getting staff to collaborate yet drawing boundaries. While I will talk more about this below, weaknesses of people management skills and internal communication seemed to be the consistent drawbacks in his skills as a leader.

Staff and departments

The museum had a typical departmental organization of an art museum with a CEO overseeing the different departments. The museum's organizational chart (see Figure 4.1) indicates that CFO was the next in the hierarchy, who also assumed the role of deputy director of operations, which included duties of HR and IT. He directly oversaw the office administrator, retail and visitor services (i.e., museum store manager and visitor services associates), facilities (including facilities manager and assistant), director of security (contracted with another company), and catering (contracted with another company). The CEO oversaw the CFO and three other primary departments of the museum: Education, Collections and Curatorial, and Development and Marketing. The staff turnover seemed relatively stable since

2012, but the development director and development staff turnover was high compared to other staff positions; there was a new development director every time I visited the museum for data collection.

In the eight years between 2011 and 2019, the museum maintained one person of color on its staff, the office administrator. More than two-thirds of the full-time staff members were women, most part-time staff members were women, and most docents (out of 60) were retired women with a few men and one person of color. Most staff members, with the exception of the facilities manager, the facilities assistant, and the office administrator, had bachelor's degrees or higher. Several staff members have come and gone, but they were replaced by professionals with similar representation and socioeconomic and educational backgrounds.

Education department

Education was the largest department in the museum having five and a half full-time staff members as well as overseeing gallery hosts (people who help orient visitors in galleries), interns, volunteers, and docents. The Education Department also managed and prepared programs and exhibitions for the family activity center and four studios. An education staff member, Eric, said the mission of the Education Department involved around one word, *relevance*. He said, "I think that's what the core of education really is. It's like a sort of interpretive arm that takes the exhibits that can sometimes be....complex....make sure that everyone feels like the content is accessible and is relevant" (Eric, personal communication, June 5, 2019). After the former head of education of 20 years left, Emily, who was first hired in 2009 as the outreach program coordinator, became the director of education. Besides Emily, the museum had an education program coordinator, creative arts coordinator, outreach coordinator, outreach educator, and part-time gallery host manager. The Education Department was the only unit that had added at least one more staff person to the team between 2011 and 2019. Additionally, some roles of education staff shifted toward more K-12 outreach to fulfill the gap of public arts education in the community.

Collections/curatorial department

The Collections Department included three full-time staff members: a collections manager, an assistant curator, and an assistant registrar/preparator. The Collections Department was located on the first floor of the museum along with security and facilities staff, while all other departments were located on the second floor. Ted, the collections manager, was hired in 2008 after having worked in the museum field for more than 20 years. While he started as a registrar, his role evolved into overseeing the entire collections and exhibitions management. He did not have traditional curatorial training (e.g., advanced degrees in art history), although some of his responsibilities included curation in working with Joe, the CEO. The museum had not had a senior curator since the early 2010s. Joe had been acting as a head curator or artistic director during his time from 2012 to 2019. He said, "Yeah, I was kind of the chief curator in a certain way overseeing stuff and I did some shows" (Joe, personal communication, June 12, 2019).

Since Joe became the director of the museum, he took a different approach to curatorial work. After dismissing an associate curator with a PhD, he hired an assistant curator who was a good communicator but was without a PhD, which is a traditional curator qualification. Ted, the collections manager, described this curator as, "She's more wide ranging in her interests and abilities so she can have a really good conversation with people about whatever the topic is in a very unselfconscious way" (personal communication, June 11, 2019). Staying away from a senior specialist curator model helped the museum to bring in more diverse exhibitions and perspectives by working with guest curators or other museums in showing new exhibitions. For example, when the museum booked a traveling show or worked with another museum, the exhibition came with a curator who worked on that show, who could act as a consultant to provide a level of detail in the specific context of the arts and artists.

Avery's direction was on par with emerging curatorial practice of the field. The recent trend is that curators' background and training are becoming more diverse and more generalist. The demand for museums to become more community-oriented, diverse, inclusive, and relevant challenges the notion that the role of curators is to distribute expert knowledge about one particular subject area. The former director of the Walker Art Center in Minneapolis, Olga Viso, asserted that with the changing climate, curators will need to learn how to share their knowledge and research with more accessibility using diverse approaches (Dobrzynski 2010). As an example, one education staff member at the Avery commented on a curator she personally knew. She said he was a curator at an art museum in a mid-sized city and he had an education background. "For that reason, every space in the galleries had some kind of educational component which made the museum so much fun" (Holly, personal communication, June 7, 2019).

Development/marketing department

Development included three and a half full-time staff members. The director of development oversaw the development officer, a membership manager, and a part-time marketing assistant. The director of development worked closely with board and committee members as one of the board's major roles was to raise money. There was frequent turnover in this position. The most recent director of development, Stacy, who came from raising funds for a large university department, was hired in May 2019. There was a complete turnover of the development team from 2012 to 2019. The museum's former grant writer, James, said it was not unusual to have a high turnover in the development field. He said, "it's a difficult job asking people for money.... Contributed income weighs heavily on the budget of many nonprofits. So there is a lot of responsibility there. It's not just the Avery that has that evolving type of [development] department" (James, personal communication, June 18, 2015). The average turnover time for development directors is 18 months (Clevenger 2017). Despite these changes, the museum had been successful in fundraising and in growing its endowment. For example, people who gave annually at a small level increased in number from 7,000 in 2013 to over 10,000 by 2019. The museum's endowment grew from about $3 million in the mid-2000s to over $7 million by 2019.

At the Avery, marketing responsibilities were part of the Development Department. Without a full-time person in charge, marketing efforts frequently fell below what was often expected by visitors and other patrons. While the position used to be full time, in recent years (2014–2019), it remained part time. Some noted that the museum needed better branding and more social media presence to attract younger audiences. The museum used social media but was not very active in using it as a marketing tool. Rather, the museum tended to utilize traditional marketing strategies such as newspapers and TV commercials as well as using an existing email list for weekly e-blasts. The new director of development recognized the need for a full-time marketing person. Not having sufficient marketing efforts and budget may be limiting who the museum can invite. A former marketing staff member said that there always was an effort by the Avery to stay within a limited marketing budget although "having a voice means money" (personal communication, July 18, 2015). The museum needed to invest more in diverse marketing efforts to invite different pockets of people from the community, especially those who were not coming to the museum.

Culture

As described above, the Avery had a great deal of director and staff turnover after the museum moved to its new location in the early 2000s. Several staff members described the two years without a permanent director (2010–2012) as "The Wild West." This captures the feeling of no direction and vision during that time and how that resulted in staff members focusing on simply getting their own work done without thinking about how their contributions related to other people and departments and the museum's function as a whole. This was right after the interim director, Deborah, minimized museum operations and Ed was the acting director. Staff longed for a long-term leader who really understood the community and what the Avery had meant and could become to the community with a clear direction. The museum's overall workplace culture in the beginning to the mid-2010s could be described as "compartmentalized" and "siloed" with different subcultures and a lack of communication and collaboration. A stable leader who stayed long term (the longest by a substantial amount in the history of the Avery

CEOs) was an important factor in making the museum's workplace culture more stable, and staff members felt that the workplace culture was better by 2019, although they also felt that it could be better. With his delegative leadership, Joe helped create an overarching cultural aura that was relaxed and hands off. However, a lack of clear communication top to bottom and among departments was a consistently cited issue. Staff also wanted more transparency in important decision-making. Additionally, consistent and formal collaboration among departments was still missing at the museum.

Subculture

One noticeable subculture of the museum that was perceived as different from the rest of the museum was the Education Department. The office administrator (personal communication, 2019) said that education staff members worked well together with each other and with respect. There was a consensus that education staff members felt that their opinions were valued and they could share their ideas freely. They noted that it was Emily's leadership style that trusted them to do their job well without micromanaging. This is in stark contrast to her predecessor who was more controlling and not open to working with other departments. An education staff member, Rebecca, said the previous education director's working style was very compartmentalized and inflexible. Emily, on the other hand, was a lot more open to talking and brainstorming casually with everyone on staff; she even wanted to hear my inputs, although I was an outside researcher. I was always welcome to sit in on the education meetings when I was visiting the second and third times when she was in charge. This was not the case during my visit in 2011 with the former head of education. One education staff member emphasized the openness of the Education Department. He said, "When I talked to Emily about an idea, she said, 'Oh, we should talk to Joe about that,' so it always feels like all doors are open" (Eric, personal communication, June 23, 2015).

Communications

The general consensus in 2019 regarding communication at the museum was that although it had improved, it was still mostly "loosey goosey," in one staff person's words, or disorganized and inconsistent. There was a communication disconnection between the board and staff members, which was supposedly filled in by the CEO. Additionally, there was a lack of communication among departments.

CEO as a communication liaison

Joe had championed creating strategic plans every three years and the museum followed through with them. One of the last things he did as the CEO before he left in 2019 was to create his third strategic plan for the next three years for the new director. He regularly communicated the plan with the board of directors and department heads. Staff members agreed that his communication was better than that of his predecessor in communicating the museums' direction and general approach in moving forward with donors and community leaders. The majority of the staff understood that he wanted the museum to be "down to earth" serving local people and artists and becoming a hub for community social interaction and learning.

However, when asked for the area of improvement for his leadership, staff almost unanimously said better communication from the top. Although Joe was good at creating an overall shared direction for the museum and communicating that with the board and staff, more detailed information sometimes did not come down to individual staff members who needed it the most. This problem was attributed to both Joe and some department heads who sometimes would "forget" to communicate. Several staff members observed that there was a lack of communication from the director to each department, creating a communication black hole somewhere in the pipeline from the director to department heads to each staff member. Information was sitting at someone' desk or inbox, not delivered to staff who needed it to successfully complete their work in an efficient manner. One upper-level staff member said that Joe was too cautious in what to share with the rest of the staff. He said, "I think sometimes information is held very closely. So we could do better as management of making sure everybody understands what direction we're going in, what issues we're dealing with" (personal communication, June 12, 2019). Another staff member felt the same way. She said,

> Certain information stops. And I agree there should be some information that doesn't trickle down but I think a lot more information could be coming down than is. It...will probably make the staff better staff. You know, it helps you put your plans in place. It helps you do your strategic planning and helps you to focus on what's best for the Avery if you really know what's going on.
> (Anna, personal communication, June 10, 2019)

Opaque hiring and dismissal decision-making processes

Another area of contention was that most staff members felt the hiring and dismissal processes were unclear. Several of them felt that the hiring process was too informal and was not rigorous enough. They longed for more transparency in hiring and dismissal decisions as it was related to their livelihoods. While the upper management did not have an obligation to share the reasons behind someone being hired or dismissed, the lack of transparency was not received well by some staff members, which affected morale. An education staff member, Rebecca, said her biggest concern at the museum was how people were just "brought in" (personal communication, June 12, 2019). One example was a former intern who became part of the team without going through the formal hiring process. She said, "things like that give me a pause" (Rebecca, personal communication, June 12, 2019). Another staff member who was "brought in" said that there was some skepticism toward her ability to do the job, feeling that her first couple of months was almost about proving that she could do the job. This indicates that an opaque hiring process can be harmful for both existing staff and new hires.

Some of the dismissal decisions at the museum over the years really made people worry about their livelihood because some of the people who were dismissed did not know why they were let go and were not given proper instruction or feedback to correct issues beforehand. For example, despite his successful record of getting grants, James, the former grant writer, had been let go. While it is a common practice to eliminate positions, how he was let go was not well received by the remaining staff. A former staff member said,

> before James was let go, he has had lunches with me several times saying 'you know, I am getting scared. I am not really sure what's going on' because when he described Joe was starting to write and slowly kind of cut James out of it....So, James kind of stopped writing all along.
> (Personal communication, July 17, 2015)

James said that he was not happy about the decision to let him go but the manner in which it happened was what bothered him the most. He said, "I was active amongst the staff and I did my job and all of a sudden my position was cut right before Christmas. Right after my wedding" (James, personal communication, June 18, 2015). Lack of transparency and effective internal communication were consistently cited as areas of improvement for the CEO and other upper management. An added concern was the fact that the museum did not have a full-time HR person who could handle complaints and improper processes of hiring and dismissing employees. As briefly noted above, the CFO assumed the role of HR but most staff found it to be insufficient and sometimes inappropriate because he was also someone who closely controlled financial matters of the museum.

Collaboration among departments

The museum previously had a compartmentalized approach to exhibitions and programs, especially during my first visit in 2011, with each department making decisions without the benefit of input from other departments. While not having a stable leader for a while caused this to be more extreme at the Avery, this compartmentalized practice to exhibition and program planning is common in the museum field. However, the industry is moving away from this model and adopting a more team-based and visitor-centered approach (Love and Villeneuve 2017).

The Avery had shown signs of collaboration among different departments by consulting with each other on exhibitions and programming during my visit in 2019. However, the collaboration was not consistent as there was no set process of team-based approach to exhibitions, programing, and marketing. Compared to 2011, the curatorial process became more collaborative at the Avery. The museum had an associate curator during my first visit in 2011, but the planning process was limited only to the curator and the Curatorial Department, where it did not share the exhibition ideas to include the Education Department or Marketing Department from the beginning. Several education staff complained that they ended up doing a lot of last-minute programming for an exhibition and did not feel the Curatorial Department was open to sharing and working together.

Informal collaboration among departments

This process has changed when Joe was hired in 2012 and he began to act as a chief curator. While Ted, the collections manager, and Joe, the CEO, made final exhibition decisions, there was more informal collaboration among staff within the Curatorial Department and with other departments. Joe said, "we usually meet with Development [and Marketing], Education, Curatorial; we meet and try to plan it out" (personal communication, June 12, 2019) when developing new shows. However, the process has not been consistently followed. The assistant curator said,

> We used to have exhibition meetings with Joe, [the Curatorial Department and the education director] where we talked through the [exhibition] schedule....I don't think we have had one of those for a little while now. It's more informal....It's not plotted down on the calendar, like, 'Oh, it's about time we get together and talk about it'.
> (Olivia, personal communication, June 10, 2019)

At my visit in 2019, the Curatorial Department more actively sought input from other parts of the museum, though the consultation was still informal. Ted, the collections manager, said,

> If there's a particular topic that I'm on the fence about...I will put it in front of Emily [director of education] and or her team and say, 'Here's this thing. Seems like it has potential. What do you think?' and if I hear back from Emily or anybody on the team that says, 'We can do X, Y and Z'.
> (Ted, personal communication, June 11, 2019)

Then, he would be more likely to pursue that topic. He continued,

> It's not that they necessarily have a yay or nay vote. But it helps me to put my feelings or ideas or opinions in perspective. Like there might be

something that I'm totally excited about. But if nobody else is excited about it, then just maybe it's not right.

(Ted, personal communication, June 11, 2019)

Curatorial Department's lack of communication

Other times communication fell short between the Curatorial Department and the rest of the museum. An education staff member, for example, talked about an exhibition that opened in 2019 during my visit and had an interactive component that had potential to be linked to more formalized education materials. She found out about it when it was being installed and about to open to the public. She described the curatorial process as "they work within themselves…we can't promote things that we don't know about" (Rebecca, personal communication, June 12, 2019). Other staff members agreed that information from the Curatorial Department was not shared well. A development staff said,

> I think Ted's [collections manager] a little protective of the artists. And I understand you don't want us contacting the artist directly, but sometimes for marketing purposes we need to contact their people for permissions and sometimes they [curatorial staff] play a little bit too much of the middle man.
> (Personal communication, June 6, 2019)

Conflicts between development and education

Additionally, others have felt that Development was not working well with other departments especially when the former development director, Lena, was in charge around 2015. An education staff member mentioned that the Development Department sometimes planned educational events but did not include the Education Department. Education staff sometimes found out just days before the actual event making collaboration extremely difficult. From time to time, this became an issue for education staff members generating a lot of stress due to lack of planning and uncertainty. Emily said, "there is that underlying fear that if we don't know everything about what's going to happen, chances are we are going to have to pick up the slack at the end…it may push some of our projects back" (personal communication, June 24, 2015). This is a good example of how lack of communication and collaboration from one department can create chaos in many parts of the museum.

Discussion

The board of directors, who is the legal fiduciary of the museum, had been seen as disconnected from the rest of the museum. As discussed above, most of them were seen as not understanding the unique management challenges and practices of nonprofit art museums and were not representative of the wider community. Additionally, the restricted board qualifications of money, skills, and influence made it difficult to recruit people who have arts, education, and nonprofit backgrounds because often these people would not have financial capacity to give. A maximum nine-year term limit without a break and lack of participation from some board members may have created an environment where board members were not active and not making relevant decisions that could have a critical impact as a community educational place. All of these elements together made it difficult for the museum to diversify the board and to be susceptible to new ideas, new members, and new practice that could help make the museum more inclusive and relevant to the wider community. Many staff members, as well as most senior level staff members, were frustrated with their lack of understanding of the museum industry, indicating the board, who makes major decisions at the organization, may not have been setting a good structural and cultural foundation for the museum to be effective, relevant, and approachable by all members of the community.

Non-networked departmental structure

The frequent director turnover prior to more permanent leadership had caused each department to work in silos, not being able to see the big picture and direction. Breaking a cycle of revolving interim directors was a great improvement for the Avery. After more permanent leadership, the museum did experience more stabilized organizational structure and strategic approaches that most of the museum actors shared. Joe's leadership also allowed staff to experiment on their own generating many innovative and nontraditional programs and exhibitions (which are topics of Chapter 5). The museum's new approach to curation was noticeable because it made accessibility and diversity a priority over a narrow and deep knowledge about art or artists by hiring a more generalist curator and inviting guest curators from other museums. The Education Department added one more staff member and expanded its role in K-12 education by shifting its internal responsibilities to meet the high demand in the community. The Development Department saw the most change in its leadership and staff members, having completely turned over from 2012 to 2019. While the fundraising effort of the museum has been successful, marketing work, which is also under development at the Avery, felt short having employed only one part-time marketing assistant. Marketing is an important mechanism to communicate what the museum does to the wider community. Due to lack of time and resources committed to marketing, the museum's marketing practice followed the traditional and status quo way of reaching to the traditional museum goers and missed strategies, such as social media, digital, and targeted marketing, for reaching out to younger audiences and nontraditional museum goers. These varying degrees of work, effectiveness, and goals of each department, without seeing how they were all interconnected, have created the museum's organizational structure to be like a broken network that is connected in some ways and disconnected in other ways.

Stabilized but stagnant workplace culture

The museum's culture has fluctuated due to change in leadership and new actors entering and leaving the museum. Based on the differing leadership and approaches to work within each department, the museum still carried on the habits of working in silos and keeping information within each department. Joe's communication efforts and reach inward have fallen short, not being able to unify varying departments to work together more consistently and formally. The lack of communication and transparency from the top to bottom influenced actors to just follow the standard pattern as it may have been seen as the "accepted" way of communicating and working. As a result, sometimes important communication stopped somewhere in the middle, not reaching the staff members who needed it the most. The most sensitive areas of communication seemed to be related to decision-making on hiring and dismissal, which affected staff morale negatively, discouraged openness, and created skepticism about people's ability to get the job done leading to less trust and collaboration among departments that already differed in working styles and cultures.

The Education Department had established solid working relationships and culture within the department under Emily's leadership based on trust and transparency. The evolving nature of the development director and staff created a situation where the Development Department did not have an established culture or consistent collaborative system with other departments which often frustrated other departments especially Education. The Curatorial Department had opened up a lot more compared to how it used to operate before 2012 and sought input from other departments on exhibition planning. However, its openness and collaboration effort was not consistent and other departments still felt that the necessary information about artists and exhibitions was not shared in order to offer cohesive exhibitions, programs, and marketing services to the public. There were no written rules on setting collaboration standards, no training, and no tangible internal incentive to work together, although the consequences of not working together were referenced repeatedly by participants. For instance, disconnection between education efforts and exhibitions (e.g., missed educational opportunity of components of exhibitions since it was not shared prior to opening) and emergencies where education staff or any other actors of the museum frantically worked to complete the project at the last minute due to the lack of prior communication and collaboration.

Mental models of throughputs

Culture and structure are manifestations of mental models of actors of the museum system over time, affecting and reinforcing each other. Mental models are like the mind of the organization while the throughputs are like the body of the organization. Like body and mind are inseparable, organizations' deeply ingrained assumptions and how they operate are inseparable. What can be extracted from the interaction among different parts of the museum's throughputs is that the overall mental models of actors were compartmentalized, not seeing the big picture and how one's action was related to others' work and their consequences. There was a clear disconnection between the board and the rest of the museum and the communication did not flow well between the two. Mimicking this pattern, connection among departments was lacking, not leading to a consistent and reliable process of exhibitions, programs, and marketing planning that were developed together from the outset and cohesive in thinking about or actually listening to the community's needs and interests. This lack of interconnection and network-based structure among the departments reflected the old way of working in silos and not sharing with each other. Once ways of thinking and working are established as the status quo of "the way we do things around here," it becomes part of the culture, making it difficult to change.

As discussed in Chapter 2, fixed and stubborn mental models developed over time are difficult to change because the organization may be stuck in a negative feedback loop. Certain levels of disruption, change in leadership and new actors, can create opportunities to see the need for a change. However, when dominant mental models are reinforced by the limited information from the internal museum system and/or from the external environment, most actors would only see the information or input that would reinforce their existing ways of doing things. This creates an "assumed form-world" (Laszlo 1972, 128), where the actors feel comfortable repeating the similar type of practices over and over without seeing any issues as they are too used to their assumed form-world. To change the dominant and status quo mental models, the system can trigger a positive feedback loop by critically examining the organization's mental models and allow the system to be more open and vulnerable to new information, ideas, and practices (Macy 1991).

Systems intelligence and system leadership

Reexamining the museum actors' fixed mental models can happen through developing a habit of thinking of themselves as part of the larger system and how their actions affect others in the system. This way of thinking is the very definition of systems intelligence. Systems intelligent actors are aware of their thinking behind any of their actions and intentionally work toward changing the thinking that could lead to change in behavior (Törmänen, Hämäläinen, and Saarinen 2016). In other words, the actors understand that they are a part of a larger system, manage their behavior in relation to the external environment, are aware of other people's actions and their effect on the larger system, and work with others to improve the larger environment (Törmänen,

Hämäläinen, and Saarinen 2016). For example, Emily displayed some of the behaviors of a systems intelligent actor who (1) understood that she was part of the larger system, which is the museum in this case, (2) was aware of how one part affected others citing consequences of failed collaboration and lack of communication, and (3) tried to improve the larger environment she was part of by promoting more collaboration within her department and with others. However, one person, leader, or department's effort without the change in mental models of all involved actors is not enough to trigger a meaningful, museum-wide positive feedback loop that can help reorganize the internal structure and culture of the museum out of stagnation.

System leadership can be instrumental in setting an environment where a system-wide positive feedback function can be triggered. As discussed above, Joe displayed qualities of a system leader in working with external stakeholders to understand how the external factors are critical in managing a successful museum. However, his qualities of an outward system leader did not translate well into internally managing the structure and culture and managing the mental models of the actors. Rather than bringing different teams together and helping them collaborate through a more unified process, he sometimes let each department handle their own problems without the input from the rest of the museum. Lack of communication and transparency in decision-making did not create a trusting learning environment where members wanted to share their ideas and inform each other's decision in achieving long-lasting and transformative changes. Joe may have understood the interconnection between the museum and its larger environment but may have neglected the interdependence among different elements within the museum open system.

References

Association of Fundraising Professionals. 2014. "Code of Ethical Standards." *AFP Code of Ethical Principles*. Amended October 2014. https://afpglobal.org/ethicsmain/code-ethical-standards.

BoardSource. 2019. "Term Limits." *Resources*. Last modified August 16, 2019. https://boardsource.org/resources/term-limits/.

Clevenger, A. 2017. "3 Reasons Why Fundraiser Turnover Is High (And What You Can Do About It)." *Bloomerang (blog)*, February 9, 2017. https://bloomerang.co/blog/3-reasons-why-fundraiser-turnover-is-high-and-what-you-can-do-about-it.

Dobrzynski, J. H. 2010. "No More 'Cathedrals of Culture.'" *The Wall Street Journal*, August 24, 2010. http://online.wsj.com/article/SB10001424052748704554104575435823569073064.html.

Gazley, B. 2009. "Personnel Recruitment and Retention in the Nonprofit Sector." In *Public Human Resource Management: Problems and Prospects*, edited by S. W. Hays, R. C. Kearney, and J. D. Coggburn, 79–92. Englewood Cliffs, NJ: Longman.

Griffin, D. 2008. "Advancing Museums." *Museum Management and Curatorship* 23 (1): 43–61. https://doi.org/10.1080/09647770701757716.

Janes, R. R., and R. Sandell, eds. 2019. *Museum Activism*. Abingdon: Routledge.
Laszlo, E. 1972. *Introduction to Systems Philosophy*. New York: Gordon and Breach.
Love, A. R., and P. Villeneuve. 2017. "Edu-Curation and the Edu-Curator." In *Visitor-Centered Exhibitions and Edu-Curation in Art Museums,* edited by P. Villeneuve and A. R. Love, 11–22. Lanham, MD: Rowman and Littlefield.
Macy, J. 1991. *Mutual Causality in Buddhism and General Systems Theory: The Dharma of Natural Systems*. Albany: State University of New York Press.
Moore, K. 1994. "Introduction: Museum Management." In *Museums Management*, edited by K. Moore, 1–14. London: Routledge.
National Council of Nonprofits. n.d. "Board Roles and Responsibilities." Accessed October 20, 2020. https://www.councilofnonprofits.org/tools-resources/board-roles-and-responsibilities.
Törmänen, J., R. Hämäläinen, and E. Saarinen. 2016. "Systems Intelligence Inventory." *The Learning Organization* 23 (4): 218–231. https://doi.org/10.1108/TLO-01-2016-0006.

5 Outputs and outcomes of museum change

Understanding of outputs and outcomes

In a museum open system, outputs are the museum's main service provisions, such as exhibitions, programs, and other activities and events. The museum's throughputs of structure and culture and the actors' mental models generate outputs. The effects—or outcomes—of outputs, such as visitor numbers and demographics and admission fees generated, are fed back to the feedback loop as inputs creating a continuous loop. Therefore, just looking at outputs in isolation from their outcomes does not reveal the effectiveness of the outputs. That is why this chapter not only examines the practices and approaches to museum outputs but also the funding mechanism that made these outputs possible and who the outputs attracted from the community as an outcome.

Efforts toward accessible and diverse programs and exhibitions

The throughputs of the Avery, discussed in Chapter 4, generated outputs primarily as exhibitions and programs. In an art museum open system, outputs are ultimately what the system contributes to its larger social ecosystem, the community. The Avery has modified its exhibitions and programs over the years to expand its target region and develop new audiences. After Joe was hired as the CEO in 2012, he increased the exhibition budget and helped bring in more ambitious exhibitions on a national and international scale. At the same time, he emphasized the importance of local arts and artists by more actively featuring them at the Avery. The museum provided typical art museum programs such as outreach programs, docent tours, lectures, and gallery talks, as well as other educational and social programs such as free family days, late evening programs with food and drink services, and art classes for adults, youths, and children. As I discussed in Chapter 4, the process of curating and programming had become more collaborative at the Avery. However, there was not an established exhibition and program team approach to create exhibitions and programs together from the outset. There have also been several initiatives and directional changes affecting programs and exhibitions at the Avery since 2011 to welcome more diverse audiences. As shared in Chapter 1, I define diversity as ways that people are different in terms of race, ethnicity, gender, sexual orientation, and socioeconomic status as well as their differing ideas and opinions.

More free admission

The admission charge was a barrier for many families and potential visitors in the area. A facility management staff member said, "There are a lot of families that can't afford it if you got three or four people. You need to think about eating out, kids seeing stuff and wanting them in the store" (personal communication, July 17, 2015). A survey participant from 2019 said the museum needed "to get admission price to be more reasonable. If the minimum wage is $7 or $8 per hour and asks $10, that turns off some people." To address this financial barrier, the museum first offered three months of free admission in the summer of 2015. After seeing the results of this initiative, the museum found a donor to fund admission charges for every summer. This change seemed to have influenced an increased number of visitors and as a result the museum offered more programs and social activities during summer. While I will go into more details of visitor compositions and changes below, the museum's visitor number has increased dramatically from 2011 to 2019. An education staff said, "We have stuff every single day during free summer, because we have the audience every single day" (Rebecca, personal communication, June 12, 2019).

Increased diversity

Staff members commented that one notable change in exhibitions and programs in recent years was that departments had diversity in mind when designing exhibitions and programs.

Collections

The museum adopted a strategic approach to increased diversity in exhibitions and programs when it realized how little its collection included works from women artists and artists of color. While the museum's collection grew over time based on a core collection that was donated by local elites and included art from different parts of the world, representation of artists in the collection was not very diverse. This is an age-old industry issue. A study found a majority of art museum collections remain white and male (Topaz et al. 2019). The study found 85% of artists represented in major US art museums are white and 87% are male (Topaz et al. 2019). Noticing this pattern in its own collection, the Avery made a conscious effort to update its acquisitions policy to collect artworks from more women artists and artists of color.

Experience

The museum has engaged in several meaningful exhibitions that featured artists of color and issues of social justice. One such artist that I had a chance to interview visited the River Cities area over the course of a year and collected stories of African Americans in the community as well as various leaders in the black community. He invited the participants, who were the source community for this specific project, to perform at the museum and to tell their own stories as part of the installation. The assistant registrar said,

> When he did them [the performances] in the gallery, it was packed. And those were probably my favorite nights at the museum thus far....We're seeking out those exhibitions that are going to make people feel included and are going to represent stories that are not just the white experience.
> (Personal communication, June 14, 2019)

Another staff member said, "that was another time in which race wasn't just a part of the side conversation, it was the conversation...that was brought up in a very overt way" (Eric, personal communication, June 5, 2019).

As seen in this example above, the museum was becoming a place where tough conversations could happen. The Avery had several exhibitions that were directly related to social issues such as racism and climate change. An education staff member articulated this role of the museum saying,

> One of the more important roles that goes beyond the basic roles of collecting and exhibiting and educating is kind of being a hub to have difficult conversations....Well, we could talk about race right now...we could talk about things like police brutality and institutional racism.
> (Eric, personal communication, June 5, 2019)

This was also shown in how other community groups used the Avery's space. For example, a Jewish organization hosted a program talking about the Holocaust, and the black history center had used the Avery to show a film about an interracial marriage and facilitate discussions afterward.

Population and culture

A recurring annual project that was popular among members of the community was the Day of the Dead celebration. It was a series of programs related to this Hispanic holiday as the Hispanic population of River Cities was growing rapidly. River Cities had two bilingual schools in South City in the South State, and most school districts in River Cities included the Day of the Dead in their curriculum. A local nonprofit leader who primarily served the Hispanic population said, "It was such a great event. And, you know, you saw many Hispanic, so many brown people....But there were so many white people there too" (Elena, personal communication, July 16, 2015). Rebecca, an education staff member, was in charge of it and worked with local Hispanic community organizations. The event at the museum became so popular that in 2018, it attracted over 4,000 people in five hours.

While this event was well received by most, some participants said it actually did not lead to black and brown people coming back to the museum for other exhibitions and programs. A gallery host coordinator commended,

> They don't really come back. So there should be more throughout the year, more inclusive activity…for groups of all different backgrounds together.…What I don't want them to do is only have you come this day and then this group of people come this day.
>
> (Personal communication, June 13, 2019)

The CFO said, "We've had some Native American stuff, African American stuff, definitely Hispanic stuff. Yeah, I think we're okay that way. Are we seeing the numbers and the visitors that represent them? Maybe not" (Ed, personal communication, June 12, 2019). There is an issue with this type of *special* approach to attracting minorities. It is treating people of color or backgrounds differently through special events, which could be seen as tokenism.

Relatable exhibitions and programs

The museum had been a lot more interested in local artists and showing what was familiar to local people. As an example, Joe (personal communication, 2019) told a story about a collection of portraits from ordinary people from a small town in the North State. Although this work was expensive to acquire and difficult to install, the museum made it a priority to purchase this work and showed it as much as possible because local people enjoyed art that they could personally identify with and saw as relevant. The fact that the Avery would purchase and show local arts sent positive messages to the community, helping change the elitist perspective toward the museum.

Broad and multiple forms of the arts

Additionally, the museum had approached exhibitions and programs much more broadly since 2011, not just focusing on fine arts or visual art. The museum's efforts to show more local art, supporting local artists, and showing arts that were not considered fine arts by many traditional museum-goers created an environment where staff felt free to take risks. For example, the museum had been experimenting more with programs mixing different arts forms. One such program that I witnessed at the museum in 2019 was a dance performance choreographed by a local performing artist. All different shapes and shades of bodies danced together followed by a poem recital.

An education staff member said, "You know, rappers and things like that were completely out of the realm....15 years ago...we would have never done that....So, that's been a big nice shift" (Holly, personal communication, June 7, 2019).

In an effort to broaden the meaning of art, the museum geared more toward what community members would enjoy and consider art. According to several visitors, the community enjoyed decorative arts and industrial crafts. One visitor said that he liked furniture exhibitions because he could relate to the material culture and practical art on a personal level. The museum continued mixing in exhibitions that could speak to many different people regardless of their backgrounds, including exhibitions related to popular culture. Joe, the CEO, agreed that popular culture shows have been a good way to draw people in who may not be traditionally interested in art museums. Referring to a popular exhibit based around a classic film, he said, "it wasn't even really an art show...but that was a real turning point in terms of our visibility and how people felt about us" (Joe, personal communication, June 12, 2019). A board member commended, "Curators might think 'OMG, what are we doing with this?' But...if it gets people in the door for the very first time...this draws them in—fantastic" (Margaret, personal communication, June 30, 2015). A local artist (2015) commented on this strategy of the museum exhibition and programming as *well balanced*. He said challenging exhibitions were often coupled with other shows or programs that were more palatable, showing the strategic effort toward serving the broader public.

Regularly scheduled blockbuster shows

Another approach the museum took was to have a blockbuster show every two years. These shows could be very expensive to book and may not even recover the cost if the exhibition was less popular. The Avery fundraised to establish an exhibition endowment of over a million dollars for this purpose so there would be an influx of cash to book large-scale, popular exhibitions every two years without a risk of accumulating a deficit. The exhibition about European masters in 2019 was a huge hit. Joe explained that the show was open for free in its last week and there was about a two hour wait. "It was crazy. I mean, it was actually ridiculous, but...it became like a thing that people wanted to do just because it was something they thought they should do" (Joe, personal communication, June 12, 2019). Some have argued that blockbuster shows were not effective in building loyal audiences because visitors to those shows would not come back for other regular exhibitions and that it requires better and more exciting shows to make the previous blockbuster visitors to come back (Schneider 2018). However, the Avery's sustainable financial approach to these exhibitions and the popular cultural nature of some of them have proven this strategy to be less risky and more approachable for the Avery.

Social activities

Some of the museum programs were more social and service oriented. The most popular program was the late evening event once a week when the museum remained open until 9 p.m. (instead of 5 p.m.) with the cafe open with food and drink services. This evening event, which started in the mid-2010s, offered a variety of activities including live music performances, docent tours, gallery talks, lectures, and/or movie viewings. Over time, it has been attracting more people. I met some young professional participants through some of these evening events. One young professional participant said that it was a great way to meet museum staff members that were not visible to the public for the most part and talk to people about art and social issues at a deeper level. While the museum's target audience for these evenings was young professionals and it was successful getting some of them, most attendees every week tended to be roughly the same group of retirees, board members, docents, and museum members.

Increased K-12 education programs

The museum was always strong in its K-12 educational programs either through in-house classes, tours, and programs or through public school outreach where educators went to schools and gave lessons. For example, the museum served more than 30,000 students annually by 2018 through its outreach efforts. The museum also had a designated endowment fund to pay for bus trips for schools. In 2019, the museum gave tours to more than 5,000 public school students. Emily, the director of education, said serving more students was a strategic move as well as filling the visual arts education gap in the public school system. She said,

> We started really ramping up the outreach because we thought if we could get the kids invested in this place, then we don't have to tell the parents to bring the kids. The kids will tell the parents to bring them. That's more powerful than any marketing tool.
> (Emily, personal communication, June 10, 2019)

Additionally, it is one of the best ways to build cultural capital (Bourdieu 1984) and make going to museums and supporting them a natural thing when they grow up (Dumais 2019); they will then bring their children to arts amenities in the future (Falk and Dierking 2000). As an anecdotal evidence, a gift shop part-time staff member (personal communication, 2015), who has worked at the Avery since the opening of the museum, said she started seeing kids who participated in museum programs as children came back to the museum for visits and even became interns.

New gallery host program

One notable change in 2018 was the new gallery host program which was under the Education Department. This program started because of frequent comments from visitors that they felt uncomfortable having security guards around in the galleries while they were looking at art. A security personnel said that one visitor of color felt racially profiled while visiting the gallery. The security director said, "When we're out there, people might feel like they're being watched, followed, or whatever the case is. The other reason is especially in my experience before the gallery host, visitors wanted information that I couldn't provide" (personal communication, June 6, 2019). To remedy some of these outward facing concerns at the museum, the Education Department suggested a new program that would have someone in the galleries to monitor (for eating and drinking in galleries and touching artwork that is not meant to be touched) and to provide information about the art and exhibitions if visitors desired. A board member said, "that [the gallery host program] was really kind of smart....We downsized our private security firm and we brought in the community gallery hosts. A lot more money saved and more human touches" (personal communication, June 14, 2019).

Toward networked and sustainable funding model

Traditional nonprofit funding models that relied too much on white, wealthy patrons have been challenged in recent years. There is a continuous debate on whether it is truly sustainable because this traditional donor group is shrinking with changing demographics (Jung 2015a). The US nonprofit system encourages organizations to fundraise, which in theory could satisfy the needs of diverse people. In other words, people can give to organizations and causes they care about instead of governments funding arts and cultural organizations uniformly as in many Asian and European countries. Some of the drawbacks of the private funding models are that there is a limited pool of people who would fund arts organizations and they tend to be white, wealthy, and well educated. When people who fund the museum are also users of the same organization, the chances of the organization's services reflecting the needs and wants of those who donate are high (Fleming 2002; Jung 2015a), resulting in serving a narrow group rather than promoting the needs of diverse people.

Reta, the former director of development during 2011, emphasized that there were not many donors who gave to the arts in River Cities. She said,

> When you look at the donor list for the nonprofits, when you go to the charity events, you will see the same people over and over again. As a fundraiser, I mean I go to a lot of those things, do I see it?
> (Reta, personal communication, July 17, 2015)

She observed a few families funding all arts and cultural amenities in town, which could lead to donor fatigue and an overall sustainability issue for arts funding. Reta shared,

> There are three siblings that are all in their 50s and 60s, very wealthy family but also very dedicated to giving back in local cities. Well, between all of them, they are involved in the Avery, the Science Museum, the hospitals, the symphony. I am sure there is more. They will literally say to me, 'Somebody else needs to step up'.
> (Personal communication, July 17, 2015)

The CFO agreed that the funding sources for the museum were not consistent saying, "When the economy is not doing well, people pull back....It goes through periods where it goes up and down" (Ed, personal communication, June 26, 2015). The Avery had identified some of these issues and limitations of a traditional nonprofit private funding model early on. Dealing with these financial and fundraising challenges, the board, Joe, and other upper-level staff members worked toward increasing the endowment, eliminating debt from building the new facility, and securing long-term government funding.

Larger endowment

One way to increase financial sustainability of nonprofits is to increase endowments. An endowment is a pool of money invested to generate consistent income. While the principle cannot be spent, the interests and dividends earned from investing the money can be used for mission-based activities, providing funds in perpetuity. The Avery started with a relatively small endowment of $3 million at the beginning of the 2000s, and it had over $7 million by summer 2019. It was a deliberate decision to campaign to increase the endowment rather than putting money into, for example, renovating the plaza in front of the museum, which was consistently cited as an eyesore by many visitors. Endowment size varies from organization to organization, but to provide a comparison, a contemporary art museum also in the Midwest that is a similar size to the Avery had an endowment of a little over $8 million as of 2019. The Avery was definitely making good progress toward enlarging its endowment. With a larger endowment, the museum could have more stability and do longer-term planning with the expectation of a certain level of income.

Elimination of debt

One of the museum's goals was to eliminate debt on the building because it was financed to cover the rest of the construction costs not covered by the city, the Avery family, and other donors. As shared in Chapter 3, the new building and relocation project ended up costing about $15 million over the initial budget. The goal of eliminating debt through fundraising was believed to be an almost impossible task. In fact, in 2015, when the museum completed a feasibility study to plan a capital campaign, the consulting firm advised against eliminating debt as one of the goals. Through focus group interviews, the consulting firm found out that eliminating debt indeed did not resonate with the donors. Joe said, "It just wasn't sexy. Some of them said the interest rates are so low, why pay it off?" (personal communication, June 12, 2019). This showed how much donors did not want to fund non-attractive, invisible expenses regardless of its importance to the actual sustainability of the museum. The museum leadership was brilliant in working against this reality by being creative. Instead of going to existing individual major donors, the museum approached a local gambling association that was supposed to give away a certain percentage of revenue to local nonprofits through grants. The museum convinced the association to get rid of the almost entire debt of the museum through a multi-year grant by the end of Joe's tenure in 2019. Joe said,

> over the last four, five years, we really focused on getting rid of it [the debt] and approached different funding agencies that we thought would be receptive to help us with that. And they were. That's been going on for a couple of years now.
> (Personal communication, June 12, 2019)

This meant that the Avery owned its building outright when the building was not even 20 years old.

New deal with the city

Having understood the importance of sustainable funding model and sources, the museum was proactive in negotiating with the city as it knew the original deal would expire in the year 2024. This initial deal entailed the city subsidizing about a third of the museum's annual operating budget. Joe and the development director at the time with the board's support decided to be proactive, meeting with the city council around the mid-2010s. When I was at the museum in 2015, the museum was very focused on this, working with the city leaders and influencers, lobbying for the deal to be continued in perpetuity.

The mayor in 2015 was unsure if he was going to support it. He said, "They signed this agreement ten years ago and…that's kind of coming to an end and they want to extend another ten years [beyond the ending date], I'm thinking 'nah' about that. Let's look at some other options" (Douglas, personal communication, July 15, 2015). His argument was that it was not fair for people who did not use the museum and had more pressing matters to worry about than to pay for the museum through their property taxes. He said, "most of them, doctors, engineers, brain surgeons, heart surgeons, tend not to live in Watertown, they tend to move with their kids to the lily white suburbs for the most part" (Douglas, personal communication, July 15, 2015). When I went back to the museum in 2019, it just successfully completed a new contract with the city and the deal was much better than what it was hoping for in 2015.

Reasons for success in securing long-term city funding

On top of the upper leadership's proactive approach to get ahead of this issue before it became a problem, the museum was successful in gaining the city support for three reasons: (1) the museum took care of the city's collection, (2) there was a help from the Arts Fund, and (3) the new mayor was much more supportive of the arts and cultural amenities than the previous one.

The most powerful argument that persuaded the city to continue funding the museum was that the museum professionally took care of the city's collection. A board member said, "They have acknowledged that we manage their art. This is not a gift [it is a contract]. They're paying us for a pretty high-level service" (Jane, personal communication, June 14, 2019). The initial agreement was clear that the city had to notify the museum one year prior to ending the financial support and take the collection back. Therefore, continuing this arrangement as a contract was for the best interests of the city. The new mayor in 2019 said,

> The art is the city of Watertown's art collection and I think we had discussions related to if…the Avery isn't going to house the art, where are we going to put it? How can it be displayed? And we realized for the good of the community, not only Watertown but the entire River Cities…how can we work on a financial plan to in fact continue that relationship well into the future?
> (George, personal communication, June 20, 2019)

The result of this analysis and discussion was to fund the museum with an escalating scale factoring in inflation increasing every five years ensuring healthy growth of the museum for a foreseeable future.

The mayor in 2019 said the agreement was a three-way partnership among the city of Watertown, the Avery and its board, and the Arts Fund. The idea behind the Arts Fund was to provide funds for base-level support to six major arts and cultural amenities of River Cities, so the few elite donors were not solely responsible for them. The Arts Fund raised money from corporations, major donors, and other entities and then simply distributed the money to organizations that would be used for general operations. The former CEO of the Arts Fund relayed that the involvement of the Fund played a large role in making the deal go through by saying,

> The Arts Fund co-signed…agreements. That way they could say to the populace, 'Yeah, we're putting money into this, but look, we're not the

only ones; we have private support also.' And so you have to understand that this is important to everyone, not just the city.

(Lisa, personal communication, June 11, 2019)

This partnership made the agreement much more palatable for city officials and taxpayers. This agreement was also part of a larger initiative where the city agreed to fund the Science Museum as well which had long been struggling with its structural deficits. This may also have made the deal with the Avery more tolerable for people who may not have been art lovers.

An executive from the River Cities Chamber of Commerce said,

The mayor deserves credit there. I think the mayor did a good job ushering that through. He got funding approved for both the Avery and the Science Museum, which is not an easy task. Aldermen did not want to do that when we started the conversation.

(Chris, personal communication, June 13, 2019)

A development officer of the Avery, Anna, talked about the mayor's support for the Avery that was visible to people. She said,

He's been very supportive of the Avery throughout his whole tenure.... He holds his mayor tables [informal lunch gatherings with influential individuals from the region] here every week. And you know that makes all the difference when you have a leader that supports you. And I have no doubt that has helped us.

(Anna, personal communication, June 10, 2019)

Homogeneous visitors

One area the museum has not made much progress is the effort to diversify its governing board and staff, which was reflected in the core visitor group. In the first ten years of the museum in its new location, it did not have a large increase in visitors. A former security director said, "I can remember when I first started here we get like one person through the whole museum a day. And it's progressed to, I'm assuming at least twenty, thirty a day" (personal communication, June 23, 2015). For the size of the museum and its target area, this still was a small number of people visiting the museum. The museum traditionally had not kept track of visitor demographic information other than the head count and where visitors were from by recording their zip code. Most visitors came primarily from the two bordering states. About 60% of visitors came from the North State, and 40% came from the South State.

Since then, the museum has been more popularized by visitors, from 70,000 visitors a year in 2011, 90,000 in 2015, and to around 120,000 by the

80 *Outputs and outcomes of museum change*

end of 2019 fiscal year due to the blockbuster show on European masters. The Avery's increase in the visitor number stands out as national museum visitor numbers have decreased. According to a report from the National Endowment for the Arts, about 24% of US adults have visited museums in 2017 compared to 27% in 2002 (NEA 2018). While it was a notable increase at the Avery, compared to other entertainment sectors, some considered it meager. For example, the former mayor in 2015 said, "You have about 100,000 visits a year yet we have 800,000 people who visit the ice skating rink [annually]" (Douglas, personal communication, July 15, 2015).

Visitor studies in 2015 and 2019

According to my visitor studies conducted in 2015 and 2019 sent out to the museum's visitor, member, volunteer, and donor lists, the demographics of this core group remained the same. The number of participants in my visitor studies increased from 187 respondents in 2015 to 375 in 2019, reflecting the trend of an increased number of museum visitors and memberships in general. I also conducted non-visitor studies to see any differences between visitor and non-visitor demographics through community-wide surveys. As indicated in Chapter 1, these community-wide surveys ended up to be not very useful because not many non-visitors responded. Therefore, I left out the community-wide survey results.

The almost doubled visitor number from 2011 to 2019 discussed above may reflect that the museum has been serving more of the same demographics, who were female, white, older, wealthier, more educated, and married or in a domestic partnership. As seen in Figure 5.1, the museum predominantly served female visitors and this trend was increasing, having more female visitors in 2019 than in 2015. The museum visitors were much whiter and older

	2019 COMMUNITY DEMOGRAPHICS	2015 VISITOR DEMOGRAPHICS	2019 VISITOR DEMOGRAPHICS
Gender	51% Female	70% Female	80% Female
Race	75% White	89% White	88% White
Age	30% 50 Years or Older 40 Median Year-Old	70% 50 Years or Older	76% 50 Years or Older
Household Income	$55,000 Median	60% with over $70,000	60% with over $70,000
Education	20% with at least 4-Y College	82% with at least 4-Y College	80% with at least 4-Y College
Marital Status	40% Married	66% Married	68% Married

Figure 5.1 Comparison of Community and Avery Visitor Demographics.

than the rest of the community. While 75% of the community population was white, nearly 90% of Avery visitors were white for both years. The next largest visitor group was Hispanic or Latino at 2.56% in 2015 and 2.58% in 2019 compared to the overall community Hispanic population of 9%. In addition, black visitors at the museum represented 2% in 2015 and 1% in 2019 while the community black population was at 11% in 2019. More than 70% of the participants in visitor studies in 2015 and 76% in 2019 were 50 years or older. The largest age group at 30% in 2015 and 35% in 2019 responded that they were between 60 and 70 years old. The visitors had higher household income than the rest of the community. Over 60% museum visitors made more than $70,000 annual household income compared to the median household income of $55,000 in the community. The educational gap was the largest, having more than 80% of visitors from both 2015 and 2019 to have at least a four-year college degree, while only 20% of the community represented that group. Avery visitors were more likely to be married or in a domestic partnership than the rest of the community. This may be related to the Avery visitors being older.

Visitor occupational background did not match that of the community (not summarized in Figure 5.1). In 2015, the largest group of 37% said that they were in professional/technical jobs, followed by 30% retired, and 6% in management. This stayed similar in 2019 with 29% in professional/technical occupations, 33% retired, and 6% in management. As discussed in Chapter 3, the largest industries of River Cities were manufacturing and healthcare with a strong presence of agriculture in surrounding rural areas. Visitor occupation in manufacturing and agriculture was almost none, having less than 2% in 2015 and 0.7% in 2019 working in agriculture and about 1.4% in both 2015 and 2019 working in manufacturing industries.

These discrepancies show a substantial disconnect between core users of the museum and the general population of the community. An only docent of color at the museum in 2019 said, "I think black people are still not coming. There are a lot of people who don't know about the museum. And they don't even think about it" (personal communication, June 13, 2019). One infrequent visitor said, "I feel like people who are in the community that are economically low status probably don't think about the Avery" (personal communication, June 16, 2015). A non-visitor participant in 2015, who had never been inside the Avery, said she could not afford to go to museums because of time and money.

Discussion

At the Avery, the museum's exhibitions and programs became more diverse and included many approaches with broader community in mind. The museum tried to soften the obvious barriers such as admission charges by offering free summer admissions and occasional free days to special exhibitions. Realizing how little people of color and women artists were represented in its collection and permanent exhibitions, it changed its acquisitions policy deliberately to collect more work from artists of color and women artists. It mounted exhibitions and hosted programs about critical social issues and tried to host special themed programs that would deem relevant to growing minority groups in River Cities. The museum also tried to increase the relevancy and broaden definitions of arts exhibitions and programs at the museum to be inclusive of different types of arts, multi-arts programs, and social activities. Offering more educational programs and outreach for K-12 students was a strategic move and thinking to increase future arts lovers from a young age before they develop to think the museum was not for them. The Education Department also adopted a gallery host program, providing a friendly presence and answering any exhibition- and program-related questions prioritizing visitor experiences in galleries. These efforts led to increased visitor numbers by almost doubling the annual number of visitors from 2011 to 2019.

Networked and sustainable funding model

The museum was successful in establishing a networked and sustainable funding model setting itself up for future success. Enlarging its endowment and virtually eliminating all debt would lead to greater financial solvency and more cash inflow for years to come. This was not an easy feat, and the museum was able to do it with proactive leadership, teamwork, and strategic thinking, although there were other internal and external factors that worked in concert with the museum. The museum took care of, exhibited, and interpreted the city's collection professionally to educate people in River Cities. The Arts Fund played an important role in lobbying for the new deal and co-signing the agreement to reassure taxpayers that it was not just public money that funded the art museum. The new mayor in 2019 supported the arts more than the previous mayor. The networked funding structure that relied on multiple funding sources supported by various actors internally and externally represents a type of outcome that helps secure the future of the museum and creates a condition where its actors could take a risk not worrying about the financial success of the programs or the whims of donors. This new networked funding structure is also critical in providing more input (diverse income sources from various parts of the community) in the future, affecting future throughputs and outputs of the museum.

Need for inclusion of the excluded population

Despite the increased number of visitors, the museum still faced the challenge of homogeneous visitors who tended to be more female, whiter, older, wealthier, and better educated, which remained virtually the same or became even more homogeneous by 2019. While I do not mean to discredit the museum's efforts to make its outputs more accessible and diverse, some of the goals of the outputs to attract more diverse visitors were not achieved. Several participants voiced that despite its efforts to diversify the exhibitions and programs, the museum was not seeing the number and composition of visitors that represented the target community members. The similar discrepancy is found on the national scale. While the US society is becoming more diverse than ever, only 9% of the minority population is visiting museums (Farrell and Medvedeva 2010). Non-Hispanic whites were still the predominant visitors to art museums, comprising about 80% of visitors (Farrell and Medvedeva 2010). Based on these data, most US museums are only useful to a small segment of the society, overlooking diverse cultures, races, ethnicities, educational levels, socioeconomic status, and age differences.

Thinking about the museum as part of the larger system, the River Cities community, the museum still served a fraction and excluded many people from the broader community. The museum's approach to more diversity in its exhibitions and programs did not necessarily encompass inclusion of "the intentional, ongoing effort to ensure that diverse individuals fully participate in all aspects of organizational work, including decision making processes" (American Alliance of Museums 2018). In other words, it did not consult the diverse community members or nontraditional museum-goers on what they wanted to see and experience at the museum. Diversity without meaningful inclusion may not have lasting impact, as shown in the homogeneous and stagnant visitor composition.

As an example of inclusion, the black visiting artist to the Avery physically went out to invite and include voices of black community members in creating his art. He understood that in order to have an impactful exhibition about the black community in River Cities, their voices should be part of creating the exhibition. Otherwise, it becomes something that is based on internal actors' assumptions, risking to isolate the very group the museum wants to include. Unfortunately, this lack of inclusion of mounting exhibitions of the source community has been repeated throughout the history. A well-known example is the exhibition, *Harlem on My Mind*, mounted at the Metropolitan Museum of Art in 1969. It was controversial due to the topic of the exhibition at what was considered a "white" museum, but the most troublesome part was that the exhibition was presented from a white perspective, largely excluding the source community's input and involvement (Jung 2015b). The Avery needs to do more inclusive and active outreach to those who do not feel they belong to the museum, not just through visiting artists or other types of "special" exhibitions and programs. The museum's practice of presenting something that the community "may" enjoy without asking for their input will not get it to the heart of all community members, and ultimately misses them in the group that enjoys the museum's outputs. In addition, treating exhibitions and programs about arts and culture diffidently from those of the mainstream creates a dichotomy of black/white, poor/rich, under-educated/highly educated, further perpetuating the mechanical thinking, the antithesis to systems thinking or intelligence.

Limits of transformation without change in mental models and throughputs

The lack of diverse board and staff is an issue because the board and staff may push for diversity in outputs from their perspective but not understand how the museum may be failing to be inclusive of community voices in the process of generating exhibitions and programs. The staff as well as the board did not represent multiple voices and needs of the community. As discussed in Chapters 3 and 4, the dearth of diversity in museum boards and staff has been well documented as barriers toward true inclusion (Janes and Sandell 2019). "Too many middle aged hyper-educated white people are going to limit the degree to which museums incorporate other points of view" (Siegel cited in Merritt 2010, 30). The museum's efforts to broaden exhibitions and programs were still based on what the staff thought the community wanted to see rather than actually asking them what they wanted. The increased visitor number showed some success but more of the same demographics could be more telling about how and who the museum attracted, indicating the throughputs and mental models needed fundamental change.

The overall mental models of the museum actors were that they "try their best" but were not changing the way they do things, not addressing a discrepancy between what they think they can do and what they actually do. For example, when I asked staff members about the homogeneous staff, they all agreed that it could be more diverse but most of them said it was not intentional. Emily, the director of education, talked about how the gallery host program was an opportunity to hire people of color who would be at the gallery greeting and helping people, but ended up not working out as planned. She said,

> Because we had to do it so quickly, we just put a call out for applications through our normal channels, which means that we were only really reaching out to the people who already knew us, and we didn't have time to make greater efforts to make sure we had a diversified pool in that. I think we did the best we could in that moment, but I was disappointed in myself that we didn't create a situation where there was more time to really get the word out and reach out beyond the people we already know.
>
> (Emily, personal communication, June 10, 2019)

Over the last eight years, the opportunities came naturally as people left, but no changes were made. In this case, the actors may see that lack of diverse staff is an issue but their practice of hiring stays the same, repeating what they have done, not leading to any change.

People who are in charge of the museum and create the outputs of the museum need to change their mental models by introducing new ideas and/or new members. When a group of people shares similar backgrounds and values, they may not see any issues in their logic because they keep reinforcing the dominant shared values of the group, not leading to any substantial internal changes. Additionally, the environment, where people are embedded in the system with other people from similar socioeconomic, racial, and cultural backgrounds, would likely affect who they hire and may not necessarily see that as a problem. An upper-level staff member said,

> We don't necessarily try to have a preference. So I wouldn't say that we have skewed our approach to try to reach out for people of color. But we also, of course, are looking for the best candidate for whatever job we have open.
>
> (Personal communication, June 12, 2019)

Through the same hiring process and recruiting from the same network of people, as Emily described in the process of hiring gallery hosts, the museum perpetuated the status quo mental model of hiring, which maintained and reinforced the status quote rather than challenging it and bringing different voices. In this process, the museum perhaps excluded a certain group of people completely out of the museum worker pool, and therefore excluding certain voices from decision-making processes related to outputs.

Toward new intelligibility and learning environment

The museum needs to revise its thinking, which would lead to changes in its structure and culture, and changing the outputs that would result in achieving the museum's intended goal of serving more diverse audiences. Through this process, the throughput system makes the learning environment within the organization that would affect the outputs to be more aligned with the actual needs and interests of the community, not what was assumed to be relevant to that population. While I will discuss it in more detail in Chapter 6, not having the proper input from all parts of the community would limit the museum's capacity to grow and to create outputs that could speak to a wider audience. The learning environment or achieving new intelligence as a whole organization that can help learn together and grow as a team was missing at this museum system, not fully triggering the positive feedback loop toward a transformational change. As seen in Chapter 2, what links the throughputs to the outputs is either the new intelligibility (leading to transformation) or the stagnant intelligibility (maintaining the status quo) which are all based on the mental models of the system as well as their internal structure and culture.

To achieve a new intelligibility or learning museum environment, its internal system has to be more open and vulnerable to accept new inputs and new data from those who the museum excluded prior. Actively seeking new information is one of the most effective ways to trigger a positive feedback loop and challenge the existing mental models and status quo ways of doing things. A positive feedback loop, then, triggers behavioral changes that depart from preestablished norms or status quo (Macy 1991), making the system learn to reorganize and fundamentally modify the internal structure and culture. A learning environment starts with an individual's systems intelligence but should eventually lead to a more collective and shared intelligence for the whole museum as one person's systems intelligence or behavior only would not lead to a more transformative and long-lasting change. New intelligibility of an organization reflects this collective form of intelligence that all organizational actors have a buy-in. To achieve this, actors must understand and listen to one another, include more diverse voices, and challenge the status quo together.

Based on analyses in Chapters 3–5, the Avery museum system most lacked utilization of system-wide positive feedback functions based on new inputs. The museum left out a certain group of population entirely from its feedback loop or system perhaps not maliciously, but through inertia, habit, or privilege. The sustained core group of visitor composition showed that the museum needs to embrace more meaningful interruption of thoughts and actors of the museum, getting new input, reaching out to different subcommunities, and transforming mental models, structure, and culture together to reach new intelligibility as an organization. In other words, it can become a learning museum that can maintain the dynamic equilibrium for years to come as an important community educational organization.

References

American Alliance of Museums. 2018. *Facing Change: Insights from the American Alliance of Museums' Diversity, Equity, Accessibility, and Inclusion Working Group*. Arlington, VA: American Alliance of Museums. https://www.aam-us.org/wp-content/uploads/2018/04/AAM-DEAI-Working-Group-Full-Report-2018.pdf.

Bourdieu, P. 1984. *Distinction: A Social Critique of the Judgment of Taste*. Cambridge, MA: Harvard University Press.

Dumais, S. A. "The Cultural Practices of First-Generation College Graduates: The Role of Childhood Cultural Exposure." *Poetics* 77 (2019): 101378. https://doi.org/10.1016/j.poetic.2019.101378.

Falk, J. H., and L. D. Dierking. 2000. *Learning from Museums: Visitor Experiences and the Making of Meaning*. Lanham, MD: Altamira Press.

Farrell, B., and M. Medvedeva. 2010. *Demographic Transformation and the Future of Museums*. Washington, DC: American Association of Museums.

Fleming, D. 2002. "Positioning the Museum for Social Inclusion." In *Museums, Society, Inequality*, edited by R. Sandell, 213–224. New York: Routledge.

Janes, R. R., and R. Sandell, eds. 2019. *Museum Activism*. Abingdon: Routledge.

Jung, Y. 2015a. "Diversity Matters: Theoretical Understanding of and Suggestions for the Current Fundraising Practices of Nonprofit Art Museums." *The Journal of Arts Management, Law, and Society* 45 (4): 255–268. https://doi.org/10.1080/10632921.2015.1103672.

Jung, Y. 2015b. "Harlem on My Mind: A Step toward Promoting Cultural Diversity in Art Museums." *International Journal of the Inclusive Museum* 7 (2): 1–13. 10.18848/1835-2014/CGP/v07i02/44483.

Macy, J. 1991. *Mutual Causality in Buddhism and General Systems Theory: The Dharma of Natural Systems.* Albany: State University of New York Press.

Merritt, E. E. 2010. "Where Do We Go from Here: A Call to Action." In *Demographic Transformation and the Future of Museums*, edited by B. Farrell and M. Medvedeva, 30–31. Washington, DC: American Association of Museums.

NEA (National Endowment for the Arts). 2018. U.S. *Trends in Arts Attendance and Literary Reading: 2002–2017.* Washington, DC: National Endowment for the Arts https://www.arts.gov/impact/research/publications/us-trends-arts-attendance-and-literary-reading-2002-2017.

Schneider, T. 2018. "The Gray Market: Why Blockbuster Museum Shows Aren't Actually Solving the Attendance Problem (and Other Insights)." *Artnet News*, April 30, 2018. https://news.artnet.com/opinion/michael-jackson-blockbusters-1275152.

Topaz, C. M., B. Klingenberg, D. Turek, B. Heggeseth, P. E. Harris, J. C. Blackwood, C. O. Chavoya, S. Nelson, and K. M. Murphy. "Diversity of Artists in Major US Museums." *PloS One* 14 (3): e0212852. https://doi.org/10.1371/journal.pone.0212852.

6 Toward a deep learning museum and paradigm shift

Mutual effects of negative and positive feedback functions of the Avery

As discussed in Chapter 2, an open system sustains itself through the feedback mechanisms that interact with its external environment. A negative feedback process stabilizes an organization, incrementally adjusting to maintain its status quo. If the museum relies on the input based on the existing visitors and people who already support and patronize the museum, it tries to stabilize the existing system or throughput to produce outputs that meet the needs of a narrow population. This way, the museum maintains how it creates programs and exhibitions, who and how they hire, and relies on the same source of input without getting equally valuable information and resources available from the environment. Then, the internal system or throughput is not networked or vulnerable enough to accept and process multiple perspectives among actors inside and outside the museum. Rather, it will take in the information that already matches the existing mental models of thinking and doing things, perpetuating the negative feedback loop over and over. Change could happen in this mechanism, but it is incremental and slow, often adjusting to meet the needs and interests of existing actors and patrons and therefore not leading to transformational changes.

Triggering a positive feedback loop intentionally requires a system to be flexible and vulnerable, thereby making it susceptible to new inputs coming from the community or an external environment. A change in mental models and its systems infrastructure or throughput—structure and culture—fuels the organization to be more open to its environment and listen to different voices. When there is a mismatch between inputs and mental models, the actors can establish new throughputs where the museum adopts cultural and structural changes. In this process, the systems intelligence of actors is key in interpreting the new information and challenging the status quo mental models of the museum based on that new input. New inputs coupled with more open and networked organizational throughputs can transform the museum to acquire a new intelligibility as an organization, which then affects the outputs of the museum to match the diverse inputs. This renewing and differentiating process, or positive feedback, is the mechanism to

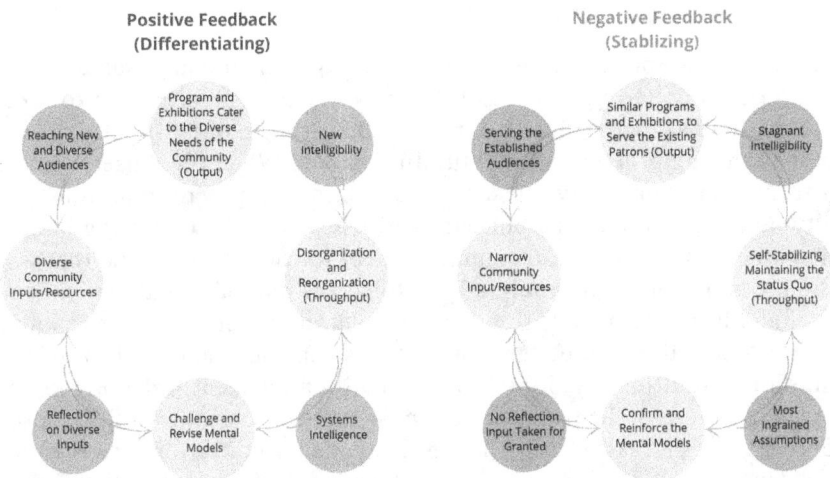

Figure 6.1 Open Systems Museum and Its Feedback Functions.

transform a museum into a learning museum that can continually learn to diversify, divert, and renew (Jung and Love 2017).

Figure 6.1 represents a conceptual model of an open systems museum and its feedback functions and highlights both positive and negative feedback processes. In Chapter 2, I introduced a basic open systems organization model (Figure 2.1) and its mutual feedback functions. Figure 6.1 is essentially the same model as Figure 2.1 but is more contextualized and specific to museum open systems and their feedback mechanisms that transform or stagnate museums. All the elements of the loop are interdependent, affecting each other in multi-directional ways as indicated in the double-sided arrows. Below, I describe input, mental model, throughput, and output of positive and negative feedback functions using specific examples from the Avery to fully describe how feedback functions work in real-life settings. Then, I will introduce an applicable model of a positive feedback function that includes leverage points for each step of the loop as well as pressure points that can be generated by external actors. Leverage points refer to an area within a system where a small change could lead to a system-wide shift (Meadows 2008), while pressure points are external circumstances where organizations are pressured to make changes in order to comply, such as change in policies, laws, and standards.

Positive feedback processes: transformation to sustainable funding model

While all elements of the feedback mechanism are interconnected and mutually affecting, I will start with the input element of the positive feedback process in explaining real-life processes.

Inputs: shrinking donor base and ineffectiveness of previous funding model

Just as the nonprofit sector in general is experiencing an issue with the old model of funding (Jung 2015), the Avery as a private nonprofit organization has experienced a shrinking donor base and difficulty raising money through the traditional funding model. When the museum made a transition from a city museum to a completely private nonprofit, the city no longer staffed the museum and its subsidy for operating budget had an end in sight. The accumulated debt for the new building that was $15 million over its original budget stifled the museum financially. Even though the museum made steady repayments and refinanced with a lower interest rate after about ten years, it was limiting the cash flow of the museum. Additionally, its relatively small endowment did not provide much cash inflow. The fact that the museum was losing its major donors but was not successful in replacing them sped up the effort to get rid of the debt, increase the endowment, and secure further city funding for the foreseeable future. For example, a board member observed that people with "deep pockets" passed away or left town, and it was difficult for the museum to replace them. The former development director echoed this point saying the museum needed a broader donor base, including more sustainable public and private funding "because a few of our top donors died in the previous year" (Lena, personal communication, June 12, 2015).

Mental models: shifting thinking behind the traditional funding model

The decrease in contributed income from major donors reduced the financial input from the community and they were not able to replace the lost funding fast enough even though there were more members and annual giving donors at a small level. Some board members and donors initially advocated for not paying the building debt off citing the low interest rate. However, other board members' expert understanding of finances served well for this museum function. Several who were financially savvy recommended the museum reduce the building debt arguing for the increase in financial freedom the museum could achieve funneling that mortgage payment toward mission critical activities. The board and upper-level staff became very aware of the finite nature of the governmental subsidy and financial constraints that came with regular debt payments and a small endowment, limiting the museum's future activities. Perhaps the financial nature of this issue made the situation more urgent and helped the actors see there needed to be a fundamental change in how the museum raised funding. In this case, the actors of the museum system clearly noticed the mismatch between funding amount and sources and the financial needs of the museum for future years;

therefore, they knew they had to do something quite soon, placing a new funding model as a priority.

Throughputs: challenging the old model of fundraising

Realizing that the existing funding model would not lead to a sustainable future for the museum, the actors of the museum challenged the old model of funding that relied on major donors and took the city funding for granted. As the city funding was about to end, it was especially critical to challenge the passive reception of funds. While the museum was utilizing other ways to increase financial input through renting out facilities and charging fees for programs and admissions, it was not enough and some of these efforts were against the museum's strategy to bring more people in by offering free services. For this challenge of establishing a new funding model, it was important to make more connections with the external actors, such as politicians, community leaders as well as new individuals and institutional donors. For effective throughput transformation that would lead to a fundamental change in funding structure of the museum, the systems intelligence of actors was required, understanding the museum as part of the community and making further connections with diverse actors, inputs, and voices from the external environment. The CEO's leadership style toward the external environment could be considered system leadership because he was deeply aware of the museum's place in the community and who to connect with to solve this problem in a sustainable way.

The process of lobbying and working with other organizations and external actors of the community was a team effort that involved the former development director, the CEO, and several board members working together. They worked very closely with local government officers and other arts and cultural organizations, such as the Arts Fund, the River Cities Chamber of Commerce, and other individual and institutional donors in creating the new funding model that is network oriented and relied on multiple actors and sustainable sources. For example, the Chamber of Commerce played an important role in lobbying the city officials and the mayor to secure the new deal. Chris from the Chamber of Commerce elaborated on the chamber's role in this effort:

> We're helping the politics of that in the background working with Alderman telling him it's not crazy. You know, the city owns the art, they'd be nuts not to….It felt expensive to Aldermen to be able to commit to that. So it took a very long time.
>   (Personal communication, June 13, 2019)

The museum worked with other funding agencies to pay off its debt and enlarge its endowment rather than relying only on major giving donors that the museum traditionally depended on.

Outputs: new sustainable and networked funding model

Through these efforts, there was a collective realization or new intelligibility of more involved actors seeing the need for the substantial change in the museum's funding model as well as how arts and cultural amenities are funded in River Cities. This new model represents networked efforts of funding arts and cultural amenities raising money from multiple sources instead of relying on the shrinking major donor groups. The immediate output in this specific positive feedback loop was the renewed contract with the city that would continue funding the museum for years to come. It not only secured the current funding level for the next five years but also would increase incrementally every five years to reflect inflation which is critical in keeping the level of support sustainable over time. This new deal required the Arts Fund to commit to continuous future funding of the Avery as well as funding the Science Museum. As such, what this deal also represented was the shift in the overall arts and cultural funding of the city relying on partnership models. This networked effort not only benefited the Avery but also other arts and cultural organizations and perhaps the perception of the publics that the Avery is not just a place for rich elites. Other outputs of the efforts toward a sustainable funding model were the near elimination of the building debt and an enlarged endowment, both of which will increase future cash inflow of the museum.

This immediate output of the efforts, a new networked funding model, has been affecting the museum's primary outputs of programs and exhibitions by being able to offer more free admissions and programs creating a potential to serve more diverse audiences from the community. Relying more on diverse sources of funding would allow the museum to work toward greater participation and be open to different ideas rather than try to please those few individuals who gave money to the organization. These outputs can lead to new inputs of donors and diverse resources encouraging and maintaining the changed model—until it is no longer working for the museum, then it will again need to go through more positive feedback function to transform it to work for a new situation, pressure, or needs.

Negative feedback processes: maintaining the status quo audiences

The financial freedom achieved from the new funding model created an environment where staff members could take risks in providing more programming and exhibitions that could depart from meeting the needs of status quo visitors. However, it had to be coupled with more changes in the internal system and mental models of those who actually create the exhibitions and programs. This internal system and mental models of actors were shown to be stagnant at the museum, which helped maintain a negative feedback loop at the Avery.

Inputs: limited community feedback and evaluations

External inputs or information the museum received were anecdotal comments from its visitors or occasional member surveys or focus group interviews for the purpose of strategic planning. For example, the assistant curator said the exhibitions were *evaluated* mainly through the comment books in the gallery. She said this method was voluntary and therefore skewed. "It's often the loudest voices that are the ones that make an impact" (Olivia, personal communication, June 10, 2019). The museum occasionally conducted member surveys, but these were for a group that was already supporting the museum, omitting other voices from the community. Participants for surveys and focus groups for strategic planning purposes were heavily based on people who were important community leaders, donors, and patrons of the museum, not representatives of the wider community. Additionally, the occasional surveys did not ask questions about basic demographic information. The development director said, "We don't have good information on who is coming to the museum....When people come to the museum if they're not members, we don't take their information" (Stacy, personal communication, June 11, 2019). This practice meant that the museum did not have diverse inputs from the community in order to understand who was coming and not coming to the museum and what the museum could do to attract people who had never visited.

Mental models: limited inputs matching existing ways of thinking

Because of the limited inputs from a select section of the community who already supported the museum, there was no mismatch between the input and the mental models that create the output that is already enjoyed by the existing audiences. This created an environment where the museum actors did not need to critically reflect on existing ways of working, thereby continuously confirming and reinforcing the fixed mental models of actors. By not actively seeking different ideas and inputs, the museum ignored the external pressures from the excluded groups and their voices. Homogeneous board and staff, who did not represent the blue-collar community population or different pockets of racial and ethnic groups, may have not known how to be truly inclusive of different voices because they did not share lived experiences with their wider community members. Some actors may have thought they were creating exhibitions and programs geared toward what the community wanted. In reality, they were working based on what they guessed the community wanted rather than what the community actually wanted, operating based on the assumed world they created.

Throughputs: stagnating structure, culture, and mental models

These conditions created an environment in which the museum's internal working systems stayed stagnant. The museum continued to work in a non-networked departmental structure, sometimes connected and other times not. As shared in Chapter 4, the museum did not have a set process of exhibition planning and program development as a team from the outset. Rather, the curatorial department or director of the museum initiated an exhibition idea, and the education and other relevant departments and actors were invited to contribute as needed. It not only did not include various actors within the museum system, but the community perspectives were never part of it. This non-networked nature and design of throughputs, reflecting the fixed mental models addressed above, did not allow maximization of receipts of new inputs and ideas. Additionally, the CEO's outward system leadership skills, which were critical in establishing the networked museum funding model discussed above, often did not get translated into creating a more effective and transparent internal system and were unable to unite disparate departments into working as a collaborative team.

Staff members could not rely on a consistent mechanism of communication from the top down, bottom up, and laterally among departments, creating further barriers to collaborative culture. Lack of communication and opaqueness in decision-making processes made the situation worse, making it difficult for the actors to trust one another and work together. The lack of communication and collaboration caused each department to determine their own set of goals that were somewhat independent of the goals of the institution and other departments. This incoherent communication system and workplace culture were reflected in how the museum communicated with its larger community, especially in terms of marketing, only reaching out to those who were already supporting the museum, not reaching out to non-traditional museum users.

Output: programs, exhibitions, and marketing

While there has been an effort to diversify its collection, artists, exhibitions, and programs, many people, especially people of color, to whom some of these programs were specifically targeted, expressed that they did not come back for other regular programs. This was something to do with the museum approaching them as "special", while at the same time its staff did not represent their community for the most part. Additionally, the museum ended up providing a variety of exhibitions and programs prepared by and presented to the core group of visitors, missing the voices of the diverse actors. As discussed in Chapter 5, despite the number of visitors almost doubling from 2011 to 2019, the visitor composition stayed the same or worse in terms of homogeneity only representing a fraction of the wider community. The visitor studies results revealed that the Avery's core visitors tended to be female, white, older, wealthier, and more educated.

Looking at marketing efforts as the museum's output in reaching the audiences, this practice stagnated by marketing to the same groups of people over time. The development officer said, "we're clearly not reaching all our demographics" (Anna, personal communication, June 10, 2019). The assistant curator agreed saying, "I think you have to do some targeted advertising and communication. Not just the same kind of things that you do. You have to find different ways to get at those audiences" (Olivia, personal communication, June 10, 2019). Another nonprofit leader commented that the museum was not marketing properly to people of color. Being a person of color herself, she felt her community was often left out. She said, "you're only putting it out to people and networks that you have a relationship already; it's a closed circle" (Elena, personal communication, July 16, 2015). The development officer confirmed that the museum marketing may be geared toward older people because most marketing efforts were newspaper advertisements, TV commercials, and physical advertisements, such as yard and vinyl signs. The museum had little social media marketing but with a part-time person in charge of marketing for the entire museum, there was a limitation in reaching out to younger people who were vastly lacking in the museum audience. Thus, there were many missed opportunities to broaden beyond their typical audience.

A negative feedback function is not always a bad thing for an organization. In fact, it is an important function of survival. However, if it is maintained and repeated too long without changing it for more fundamentally different ways to meet the changing needs and interests of external factors then it becomes disconnected from the majority of external actors or the diverse publics. As seen from Chapters 3–5, there have been some positive changes at the museum but they were not transformative enough to affect the museum's outputs as well as who was included in the process of creating, who the outputs attracted, and who the museum reached out to. This negative feedback loop continued and was perpetuated over time, making it difficult to change or see it as an issue while the museum's feedback loop completely left out the majority of publics other than a few—white, older, wealthier, more educated, and socioeconomically advantaged.

Leverage points of a positive feedback function

A positive feedback function can start anywhere in the loop, but each step can have leverage points where making changes in some places would have more lasting and system-wide effects. I will highlight leverage points in some of the elements within a feedback mechanism.

New inputs

Receipts of new inputs can enable actors to see the disconnection between the input and internal throughputs and/or outputs. The actors can still ignore the new inputs, but if they do not receive them at all, the chances to see the need for transformation are slim. There can be many inputs to museum systems, like artworks, knowledge, human resources, and money. The most important leverage point in this element is to receive information from and about the community as a whole. Two of the most effective ways to get community inputs are through visitor and non-visitor studies and evaluations of the programs and exhibitions. To get new and differing information, the museum must get information not only from existing visitors and patrons but also from people who do not visit the museum. Silverman and O'Neill (2004) emphasize the importance of visitor studies that enable museums to understand complex patterns of museum visitors, provide perspectives that reveal the blind spots in museum practices, and find new ways to engage more diverse audiences. Conducting a non-visitor study is critical for a museum in order to find out who is not coming to the museum and why, therefore allowing it to attract members of the non-visitor population to the museum (Linett, Patton, and Gariba 2011).

The Children's Museum, located in East City, a suburb of Watertown, provided a great local example of how having new input affects the internal museum practice in a substantial way. The director of the Children's Museum shared in 2015 that her museum did visitor and non-visitor studies to gather more information on what people liked about the museum and if they were not coming, it wanted to know why. Through the non-visitor studies, the museum found out that people thought they could not visit the museum unless they lived in East City. The fact that the museum was part of the East City local government caused this confusion, but the museum had no idea. The museum needed to educate its regulars as well as people who did not visit because of misinformation.

The exhibitions and programs should start with some concrete markers of success that can then be measured during and after the programs and exhibitions, collecting inputs that can be used to improve them in the way they were intended. This is a sustainable, effective way to ensure programs and exhibitions, the primary outputs of museums, are goal oriented and targeted and improve continuously. Museums must intentionally put resources behind evaluation—collecting data, analyzing, and summarizing the results—so the results can be easily digested and used by all staff members. At the Avery, there was no museum-wide system that could evaluate the museum's exhibitions, programs, and events in a cohesive and systematic way. Rather, it was up to each department to do it if and when they wanted and/or were able to do it. This type of evaluation is not useful as one department cannot implement effective and impactful changes without the support of other departments. Conducting consistent, objective, and scientific evaluations of exhibitions and programs is not an easy feat because it takes time and expertise. This may create an opportunity to hire a consulting firm or a part-time researcher or work with local academics and graduate students.

Reflection and challenging mental models

Often audience research and evaluation results are not reflected upon, discussed, used, shared, or applied among museum professionals (Korn 2017). Reflection can be an effective leverage point because without reflection and application of the research, receiving new inputs becomes a wasteful exercise. Reflection links the new community input—visitor and non-visitor studies and evaluation results—to initiate the process of challenging and revising the mental models of the actors. In positive feedback, new information coupled with deep reflection of the data can point out the mismatch between the information from the community and internal mental models, providing an opportunity to challenge the deeply ingrained assumptions and ways of doing things. Korn (2017), an evaluation consultant, developed the model of intentional practice, focused on evaluation and reflection in relation to the impact an organization aims to achieve, after she encountered the mental models of her clients showing a very linear, unidirectional, and compartmentalized view toward museum work. Staff members may see what they do as disconnected from what other staff members or departments do or what the museum has done in the past (Korn 2017).

Once the museum has more diverse inputs from the community and reflects on them, they can start challenging and revising the mental models of actors. Simply put, people have to rethink their old ways of thinking and doing things and avoid the attitude, "We do this because we always have done it this way." Changes in thinking and acting together can transform the museum actors' mental models leading to collective and cultural change. Behavioral changes that no longer support the preestablished norms are critical in internalizing the positive feedback function (Macy 1991). However, "changing personal and organizational behavior is hard because people really do not want to change; they like things just the way they are" (Korn 2017, 55). To overcome this inertia, people must embrace systems intelligence.

Embracing systems intelligence

The fixed mental models that want to maintain the status quo will create the assumed world where what they do is *always* effective. Korn (2017, 56) said when staff members are asked to rank their programs,

> staff invariably plot their programs as having high impact and using low resources. If all museum programs used as few resources and had as high impact as staff led themselves and others to believe, then there would be nothing more to learn about museum practice—because the field has already reached nirvana.

This is the danger with fixed mental models and assumptions. Without new input and the willingness to change, it will stay the same "because it is always easy for the human mind to rationalize" (Korn 2017, 57). Museum actors can overcome some of these attitudes by practicing thinking in systems ways; systems intelligence is a tool for that.

Systems intelligence is a specific capacity for one to understand his or her stance in relation to other people and within the larger system (Törmänen, Hämäläinen, and Saarinen 2016). Systems intelligence is based on the concept of systems thinking (Senge 1990) that views all parts of the world or any phenomena are interconnected to and interdependent with each other and nested within a larger whole. Hämäläinen and Saarinen (2007) critiqued systems thinking stating that the specific reason that systems thinking often did not lead to practical changes within actual relationships or organizations is that it did not address the behavior generated by the system that needs changing. Built on systems thinking, systems intelligence emphasizes one's thinking behind their action to intentionally alter the thinking and therefore their micro-behavior. Systems intelligence, therefore, is the ground-level application of systems thinking for actors to transform their action through micro-behavioral changes affecting the whole system (Sasaki 2017).

By understanding that one is part of the larger environment, she can act with sensitivity in thinking about how her action affects others and the larger system, what other people think, and how she, in collaboration with other people, can improve the larger environment (Törmänen, Hämäläinen, and Saarinen 2016). Systems intelligence can also help one to perceive other people's mental models, "identifying where people are connected or disconnected from others who must be part of the solution" (Kania, Kramer, and Sense 2018, 18). In this process, the actors can identify how their actions have been helping or not helping, how others have been effective, and what and who is missing, identifying ways to change the system in creating more effective outputs. This is where action happens; members of a system work together through a network-based model of collaboration and inclusion through micro-behavior changes.

Disorganization and reorganization of throughputs

By embracing systems intelligence, the museum can establish a more networked working culture and environment. One of the important aspects of operationalizing inclusiveness, which is an important leverage point of throughput transformation, is through inquiry and active listening to learn from differing viewpoints and making that a priority by intentionally allocating time to do it (Korn 2017). Communication is essentially how new information is shared and discussed, helping members of an organization work toward the same goal. Intentional and inclusive communication systems can help provide more opportunities for active listening and asking questions. "It is through asking questions that an individual gains awareness, clarity, and deeper levels of appreciation and understanding of others' points of view" (Korn 2017, 57). Senge, Hamilton, and Kania (2015) describe this type of inclusive communication as generative conversation where actors can "try on" different perspectives and ideas from others. In this process of trying on new ideas and asking questions, the actors question, revise, and release their ingrained and stubborn assumptions that would not be useful in solving complex problems (Senge, Hamilton, and Kania 2015).

Cultural change alone cannot transform the museum as it can easily fall back to the way it always has functioned. So, these ongoing efforts of cultural change need to be accompanied by structural changes that would support, maintain, and renew the culture as well as continuously support the positive feedback loop. Leadership is critical in creating an environment where fixed mental models are challenged and new ways of communicating and working can be internalized in the museum structure. On a leadership level, systems intelligent leaders can help establish an inclusive environment that appreciates and encourages diverse voices and perspectives in being heard (Senge, Hamilton, and Kania 2015).

Another structural area of a leverage point is to create, revise, and implement policies that would reflect new culture and practices leading to systemic change of the overall museum practices. While policy change has potential to set the tone and goals for the museum that all staff and leadership can get behind, policy that is not communicated or lack of policy in certain areas can have a negative effect such as inconsistent hiring and dismissal decisions, which discouraged morale and further collaboration as seen at the Avery. Policies in this area can also help the museum to get out of the old way of hiring people based on the existing pool of candidates. Through a more transparent process of hiring and dismissal set as a policy and shared with all actors, museums can add new actors who may not share the same assumptions and backgrounds and perhaps represent those who the museum wants to attract but are not yet coming.

These cultural and structural dis- and re-organizations, coupled with changed mental models and new actors with differing voices, can create an environment where a museum can establish a networked structure, a multi-directional communication system, and collaborative working style. These conditions help transform museums to achieve new intelligence as a whole or a learning organization that continuously grows and learns to be better, maintaining the state of dynamic equilibrium (discussed in Chapter 2). The state of dynamic equilibrium describes an inter-state of a system that is always prepared to make changes depending on inner and external pressures rather than staying stagnant or chaotic (von Bertalanffy 1950). In my mind, this state is always accompanied by a sense of excitement and a healthy dose of urgency.

New outputs: sustainable differentiation thought inclusion

After transforming throughputs and fixed mental models and becoming a learning museum, museum actors can generate more diverse outputs to support the diverse inputs. The main museum outputs of exhibitions and programs can be more diverse based on a more inclusive development process that engages a variety of people and their perspectives from many parts of the community. Marzio (1991) suggested museums adopt a more inclusive approach in exhibitions and programs related to minority arts and cultures by including voices from the source communities and treating them as equal status exhibitions rather than special. Additionally, creating special programs that appeal to specific cultural groups is considered time-consuming and not cost-effective for a museum to continue year after year (Marzio, 1991). As indicated from the Avery visitor demographic survey data, the audiences who attended special programs did not necessarily return to the museum for more general exhibitions, programs, and events and they certainly did not constitute core museum visitor, donor, and volunteer groups. Diversity without inclusion does not work. And inclusion cannot happen without seeking out people who really understand the marginalized views and different perspectives. Museums need a more established collaborative culture and communication system that allows multiple perspectives to be heard and reflected in the process of creating services. This is again why museums need to diversify their board and staff in order to understand these lived experiences. The inputs received in the process of inclusion are fed back to the positive feedback loop that continues the process.

Creating external pressure points: environmental change

Although the changes within an individual museum and its community are important, the larger professional environment for museums can also have an impact. As I discussed in Chapter 2, museums as nonprofits—or public organizations in some cases or other parts of the world—are obliged to serve the diverse publics' needs and interests. Especially for nonprofit museums in the United States, their "publicness" should be reflected in their practice that comes with the tax exemption, acting as indirect governmental subsidy, and tax deduction enjoyed by their donors, acting as a tangible incentive to donate to nonprofit organizations. On a more professional level, museums are held accountable for their practice by professional organizations, such as the American Alliance of Museums (AAM) and Association of Art Museum Directors (AAMD), and their public and private funding agencies and foundations. By transforming the professional standards and policies of these external organizations, a necessary environment for museums to trigger a more possessive internal feedback loop can be created which can lead to more impactful and lasting effects. I discuss three ways to stimulate the professional environment, ultimately providing an opportunity to transform the local museum practices.

Revising professional standards: making DEAI priority

The AAM has been vocal about pointing out the importance of the educational aspect of museums, in explaining museums' role in serving the wider population (Hirzy 1992). It also published a DEAI (diversity, equity, access, and inclusion) report in 2018 acknowledging inequitable and unjust museum histories and laying out definitions of important terms and strategies to apply in order "to jump-start the long-term processes that effective DEAI work requires" (2018, 3). Bunch's essay entitled "Flies in the Buttermilk: Museums, Diversity, and the Will to Change," originally written in 2000, vividly describes the homogeneous museum workforce, lack of concern for this issue from most museum professionals, and assumptions to believe that there are simply no qualified and interested museum professionals that are of color (Bunch 2019). Twenty years ago, he said, "I confess, I am worried. Worried because after more than twenty years in this field, I am still hearing some of the same debates and conversations" (Bunch 2019, 8). And here we are; we are still talking about this. He suggested, "Our institutions would change more quickly if the development of a more diverse staff were one of the elements that contributed to the granting of accreditation" (Bunch 2019, 7).

The AAM does not use board and staff diversity as one of the considerations for accreditation. In fact, museums applying for AAM accreditation do not even have to prove they practice toward inclusivity (Coleman 2018). While the practical implementation must be well thought out so it does not become a checking box activity, it is disheartening to see how the AAM, which is supposed to be vocal about the importance of DEAI in museum practices, would accredit museums with all white boards and staff. This is a powerful tool the AAM has to influence the field in a tangible way. A more encouraging example is the Academy of Motion Picture Arts and Sciences' (2020) new standards for Oscars® eligibility in the Best Picture category to achieve equitable representation of the people involved in the making of movies on and off screen. It specifically laid out the eligibility standard that is clear and measurable in all categories of involvement, such as on screen representation and creative leadership and project team.

Some of the policy changes of professional museum associations that happened due to the pandemic have already proven to be impactful. For example, the AAMD recently loosened its stance on deaccessioning policy. Previously, museums were demonized when they sold off their collection to pay off debt or spend it in any other ways other than for buying new works or caring for existing collections. The pandemic put unprecedented financial pressure on many museums as well as a public demand for internal changes to be more inclusive. The AAMD (2020) decided to look the other way ("will not impose censure or sanctions") if museums decided to sell a part of their collection to survive and change with the external pressure to transform museums. For instance, the Everson Museum of Art in Syracuse, NY, sold its main attraction of a Jackson Pollock painting to purchase works by women and artists of color (Kinsella 2020). This shows how the professional and higher level policy changes can cause transformational changes in museums at a local level. While I have a mixed feeling about deaccessioning in general (it is a controversial topic in the museum world), the Everson's initiative shows a structural change within its internal workings.

Funding linked to diversity

Museums get public funding other than the built-in subsidy as tax exemptions due to their status as nonprofits. Federal government agencies (e.g., the National Endowment for the Arts and Institute of Museum and Library Services) and many state and local governmental agencies give grants and contracts to museums. Moreover, there are many private foundations that give grants to arts and cultural organizations. Money holds power, so funding agencies, both public and private, can put specific guidelines for organizations to meet certain diversity thresholds or to show evidence of inclusion in their work to be eligible for funding. This is not a new idea. The City of New York released its first-ever comprehensive cultural plan (CreateNYC 2017) that tried to address inequities of arts funding and access among arts institutions and artists (Boucher 2017). Based on this cultural plan, the mayor of New York City had announced that the city's arts and cultural funding would be restructured based on the organization's abilities to promote diverse arts, serve diverse audiences, and represent the diversity of their community in their staff and leadership. Recent report on this plan shows it did not really work as it intended because the demographics of the cultural workers had not changed (still whiter and more privileged than the community population) (Bahr 2020). It was considered to be ineffective because of the poor execution of the plan. The policy did not set measurable metrics organizations that received the funding had to prove; rather the organizations simply had to present a plan to meet their diversity goals (Bahr 2020). A good idea behind a policy must accompany concrete plans for implementation and evaluation, which seemed to have been lacking in this initial plan.

More equitable funding structure for arts and cultural organizations

As the Avery has achieved its new funding model, other museums could move toward network-based funding models rather than relying on a traditional fundraising model of nonprofits that relies on a limited number of major donors (either people or organizations) to fund their operation. This traditional model is not sustainable and could risk organizations drifting from their mission to meet the needs and interests of a few powerful donors. There are examples that use a wider, larger network to generate financial support for valuable arts and cultural amenities. For example, the Detroit Institute of Arts receives nearly two-thirds of its operating budget ($25 million out of $38 million) from Detroit taxpayers in three surrounding counties (Rahal 2020). In return, residents from these counties do not pay admission fees when they visit the museum while people outside of the counties will pay admission charges (Rahal 2020). Another example is the Bravo Greater Des Moines, a collaboration among local governments and private and nonprofit organizations to provide sustainable funding and community leadership to the arts and cultural amenities by raising funds from a portion of hotel-model tax revenue (Bravo n.d.). It is a good example of getting over compartmentalization in funding important amenities most people enjoy, which could be applied to transform funding models for most museums in this country.

Discussion

The general model of a positive feedback function above emphasized leverage points and external pressure points for creating an urgent and pressing environment for museum practices to transform. To trigger a positive feedback loop, the most important point that many museums miss is to receive new inputs from their community as a whole, not just from those who already use the museums. I cited two major ways museums can collect inputs: visitor and non-visitor studies, and evaluations of exhibitions and programs. However, just collecting these alone will not lead to changes. Through reflection, museum actors can identify any discrepancies between the information they received and their practice, seeing the need for change. This has the potential to transform fixed and stubborn ways of thinking and doing that are no longer effective.

Even with receiving new inputs and reflecting on them, inertia is difficult to change because people tend to go back to their old ways of thinking and doing although their environment calls for something different. The actors must embrace and practice systems intelligence to understand how their thinking and actions affect other parts and members of the system as well as overall practice. Systems intelligent leaders can help create an inclusive environment and unify members to reflect and challenge their ingrained mental models together. What makes the transformation of mental models more effective is to create an organizational structure and culture that can support new thinking and practices, thereby creating exhibitions and programs through a networked team that includes a variety of people inside and outside the museum. Hiring people who may have not been traditional museum workers through more equitable hiring practices and policies can accelerate the process of change.

These internal leverage points can be more effective and encouraged if the external factors create a necessary environment for museums to change. Professional organizations, like the AAM and AAMD, can create policies and standards that could require museums to comply. The AAM as the largest museum network and accreditation body can use its power to include diversity components with measurable and tangible criteria for museums to have in order to get accredited. Government and private funding agencies can demand museums that receive funding from them to be more diverse and inclusive by linking funding to diversity and set tangible and measurable criteria to evaluate their success. Lastly, rather than relying on a traditional funding model from a few powerful major donors, museums can establish more equitable and network-based funding models from more varied public funding sources as well as private supports so museums do not have to cater to a limited and privileged population of their communities.

These internal leverage points and external pressures could help the Avery. The Avery attempted to transform itself from an elitist organization to a more inclusive and community-based institution. The museum made many changes over the years. For example, its culture became more stable, communication was better, and people started working together more. The museum had a long-term leader who understood the museum's place within its community and worked with many external organizations, stakeholders, and actors. Its newly established funding model is notable as it created a financial stability and environment for future success where museum actors could take risks and create outputs that can speak to wider audiences as it did not rely only on a few powerful elite donors. However, some of the internal changes were too incremental and the actors still repeated traditional ways of managing, communicating, working, and hiring. The exhibitions and programs became more diverse and approachable, but its core users remained the same, continuing to serve a very small privileged section of the local population—female, white, older, wealthier, and better educated. This indicates that there was a limitation to transformation when the internal structure and culture and the actors' mental models are not changed and do not reflect the wider community they wanted to serve. These fixed mental models and practices created an inertia or repeated a negative feedback function of maintaining the status quo at the museum. To trigger a positive feedback function of the system that disorganizes, reorganizes, and renews, the museum needs new inputs through collecting data from the wider community, as discussed above. It needs to welcome new and diverse workers, establish networked structure and culture to receive new ideas and inputs, and challenge the workers' status quo mental models. Continuously practicing a positive feedback loop can transform a museum to become a *deep learning museum*.

Becoming a deep learning museum

Museums have long relied on incremental change models—making small changes and adjusting existing practice a little bit at a time (Janes and Sandell 2019). Museums are repeatedly called out on their history and practice of racism and elitism (McGlone and Smee 2020). Even with the many diverse ideas for exhibitions and programs many museums have implemented, museum visitors remain white, affluent, and better educated. Museum scholars and practitioners have criticized the lack of diversity in all museum ranks and visitors for decades. For substantial changes to happen, this incremental change model should be replaced with more radical and dramatic change models addressing the museum's internal culture and structure (Janes and Sandell 2019).

The museum field desperately needs a change theory that can be effective and long-lasting. Applying open systems theory and feedback functions based on the concept of mutual causality, fully discussed in this chapter, can help museums transform in a radical and dramatic way. The idea of a museum that (1) is capable of understanding its interconnection with its surroundings, (2) is governed by the board that represents the community and understands the values of museums, (3) has a networked and flexible internal structure to work collaboratively and listen to diverse voices from inside and outside the museum, (4) is not afraid of disorganization and reorganization even if that means changing its ways of thinking and doing things, and (5) pays attention to not only the types of programs and exhibitions and number of visitors they attract but also the process of how they are created and who were included. The actors of this ideal museum are systems intelligent, reflecting on not only their own work but also how their thoughts, actions, and work affect other actors and parts of the museum and think about ways to improve together for the greater good of the museum and its community. They actively listen to each other, ask questions, share information, and collaborate with each other. I call this ideal museum *the deep learning museum*.

Deep ecology is a comparative concept to dependent co-arising in Buddhism and emphasizes the inescapable interconnection we all share (Macy 1991; Naess 1973). I talked about the concept of a learning museum in this book and elsewhere (Jung and Love 2017). Borrowing Senge's (1990) term of a learning organization, in this *learning museum* internal actors continuously learn together to become more relevant, diverse, inclusive, and continuously remain susceptible to change to meet future challenges. The reason I qualified learning museum with "deep" is to emphasize what the most impressive museums may be missing, the genuine understanding of interconnection or mutual interdependence between museum workers and the whole museum, mental models of museum actors and the exhibitions and programs they create, the museum and its environment, and the list goes on.

The biggest barrier toward becoming a deep learning museum is the deeply ingrained and stubborn mental models of museum actors that resist change and go back to old ways of doing things out of habit without critical examination. So, what they create reflects these fixed mental models and ways of doing things. As the Buddha taught, liberation does not come from freeing one's mind from the body. True liberation or transformation comes "not through setting itself apart from phenomenality, but increasing its awareness of it" (Macy 1991, 155). The museum actor's mental models or minds are inseparable from that of the museum, and their mental models are reflected on what they create (exhibitions and programs). Therefore, a museum cannot set itself apart from its community, including previously excluded groups of community, but should increase its awareness of them through gathering more information from and actively reaching out to them.

Embracing this concept of deep learning museum has a potential to transform the museum field and toward a paradigm shift in museum practice.

When a problem is no longer solvable (repeatedly trying to diversity programs and exhibitions, but the core visitor groups remain the same) from a mental context or paradigm where the problem was created, it is time to shift that paradigm to try something different.

References

AAM (American Alliance of Museums). 2018. *Facing Change: Insights from the American Alliance of Museums' Diversity, Equity, Accessibility, and Inclusion Working Group*. Arlington, VA: American Alliance of Museums. https://www.aam-us.org/wp-content/uploads/2018/04/AAM-DEAI-Working-Group-Full-Report-2018.pdf.

AAMD (Association of Art Museum Directors). 2020. "AAMD Board of Trustees Approves Resolution to Provide Additional Financial Flexibility to Art Museums During Pandemic Crisis." *(Press Release)*. April 15, 2020. https://aamd.org/for-the-media/press-release/aamd-board-of-trustees-approves-resolution-to-provide-additional.

Academy of Motion Picture Arts and Sciences. 2020. "Academy Establishes Representation and Inclusion Standards For Oscars Eligibility." *News*. September 8, 2020. https://www.oscars.org/news/academy-establishes-representation-and-inclusion-standards-oscarsr-eligibility.

Bahr, S. 2020. "Is New York's Arts Diversity Plan Working? It's Hard to Tell." *New York Times*, August 26, 2020. https://www.nytimes.com/2020/08/26/arts/design/diversity-new-york-culture-plans.html.

Boucher, B. 2017. "New York's Cultural Plan Aims to Boost the Arts, and Diversity, in a Gentrifying City." *Artnet News*, July 20, 2017. https://news.artnet.com/art-world/new-york-cultural-plan-arts-gentrification-1027745.

Bravo. n.d. "About Bravo." *Bravo Greater Des Moines (website)*. Accessed November 13, 2020. https://bravogreaterdesmoines.org/.

Bunch, L. G. 2019. "Flies in the Buttermilk: Museums, Diversity, and the Will to Change." In *Diversity, Equity, Accessibility, and Inclusion in Museums*, edited by J. B, Coles and L. Lott, 3–8. Lanham, MD: Rowman and Littlefield.

Coleman, L.E. 2018. *Understanding and Implementing Inclusion in Museums*. Lanham, MD: Rowman and Littlefield.

CreateNYC. 2017. *CreateNYC: A Cultural Plan for All New Yorkers*. New York: Department of Cultural Affairs. https://createnyc.cityofnewyork.us/wp-content/uploads/2019/08/CreateNYC_Cultural_Plan.pdf.

Hämäläinen, R. P., and E. Saarinen. 2007. "Systems Intelligence: A Key Competence in Human Action and Organizational Life." In *Systems Intelligence in Leadership and Everyday Life*, edited by R. Hämäläinen and E. Saarinen, 39–50. Helsinki: Helsinki University of Technology.

Hirzy, E. C., ed. 1992. *Excellence and Equity: Education and the Public Dimension of Museums*. Washington, DC: American Association of Museums.

Janes, R. R., and R. Sandell, eds. 2019. *Museum Activism*. Abingdon: Routledge.

Jung, Y. 2015. "Diversity Matters: Theoretical Understanding of and Suggestions for the Current Fundraising Practices of Nonprofit Art Museums." *The Journal of Arts Management, Law, and Society* 45 (4): 255–268. https://doi.org/10.1080/10632921.2015.1103672.

Jung, Y., and A. R. Love, eds. 2017. *Systems Thinking in Museums: Theory and Practice*. Lanham, MD: Rowman and Littlefield.
Kania, J., M. Kramer, and P. Senge. 2018. *The Water of Systems Change*. Seattle, WA: FSG. https://www.fsg.org/publications/water_of_systems_change.
Kinsella, E. 2020. "A New York Museum Is Selling Its Only Jackson Pollock Painting at Christie's to Fund Acquisitions of Work by Women and Artists of Color." *Artnet News*, September 3, 2020. https://news.artnet.com/market/christies-will-sell-trophy-jackson-pollock-painting-october-evening-sale-1905985
Korn, R. 2017. "Intentional Practice: A Way of Thinking, a Way of Working." In *Systems Thinking in Museums: Theory and Practice*, edited by Y. Jung and A. R. Love, 49–58. Lanham, MD: Rowman and Littlefield.
Linett, P., C. C. Patton, and C. Gariba. 2011. "Non-Visitor Studies: Researching the Needs and Experiences of New Audiences." Panel Discussion at the 24th Annual Visitor Studies Association Conference: Sustaining a Community of Learners, Chicago, IL, July 2011.
Macy, J. 1991. *Mutual Causality in Buddhism and General Systems Theory: The Dharma of Natural Systems*. Albany: State University of New York Press.
Marzio, P. C. 1991. "Minorities and Fine-Arts Museums in the United States." In *Exhibition Cultures: The Poetics and Politics of Museum Display*, edited by I. Karp and S. D. Lavine, 121–127. Washington, DC: Smithsonian Institution.
McGlone, P., and S. Smee. 2020. "Coronavirus Shutdowns and Charges of White Supremacy: American Art Museums are in Crisis." *Washington Post*, October 12, 2020. https://www.washingtonpost.com/entertainment/museums/american-art-museums-covid-white-supremacy/2020/10/11/61094f1c-fe94-11ea-8d05-9beaaa91c71f_story.html.
Meadows, D. H. 2008. *Thinking in Systems: A Primer*. White River Junction, VT: Chelsea Green Publishing.
Naess, A. 1973. "The Shallow and the Deep, Long-Range Ecology Movement. A Summary." *Inquiry* 16 (1–4): 95–100. https://doi.org/10.1080/00201747308601682.
Rahal, S. 2020. "DIA Millage Passes in Wayne, Oakland, Macomb Counties." *Detroit News*, March 10, 2020. https://www.detroitnews.com/story/news/politics/2020/03/10/detroit-institute-arts-renewal-millage-election-results/4954684002/.
Sasaki, Y. 2017. "A Note on Systems Intelligence in Knowledge Management." *The Learning Organization* 24 (4): 236–244. https://doi.org/10.1108/TLO-09-2016-0062.
Senge, P. 1990. *The Fifth Discipline*. New York: Currency Doubleday.
Senge, P., H. Hamilton, and J. Kania. 2015. "The Dawn of System Leadership." *Stanford Social Innovation Review* 13 (1): 27–33. https://ssir.org/articles/entry/the_dawn_of_system_leadership.
Silverman, L. H., and M. O'Neill. 2004. "Change and Complexity in the 21st-Century Museum." *Museum News* 83 (6): 36–43.
Törmänen, J., R. Hämäläinen, and E. Saarinen. 2016. "Systems Intelligence Inventory." *The Learning Organization* 23 (4): 218–231. https://doi.org/10.1108/TLO-01-2016-0006.
Von Bertalanffy, L. 1950. "The Theory of Open Systems in Physics and Biology." *Science* 111 (2872): 23–29. https://science.sciencemag.org/content/111/2872/23.

Appendix A
List of key participants' pseudonyms and their affiliations

Anna	Development officer
Chris	Director of downtown development at the River Cities Chamber of Commerce
Deborah	Board member and former interim director of the Avery
Douglas	Former mayor of Watertown during 2015
Ed	Chief financial officer
Elena	Director of a local Hispanic nonprofit
Emily	Director of education
Eric	Creative arts coordinator
George	Mayor of Watertown during 2019
Holly	Outreach coordinator
James	Former grant writer
Jane	Board member
Joe	Chief executive officer
Josh	Former development director prior to 2011 and director of a local K-12 education nonprofit
Ken	Former chief executive officer
Lena	Former development director during 2015
Lisa	Former director of the Arts Fund
Margaret	Board member
Noah	Assistant registrar and preparator
Olivia	Assistant curator
Patricia	Board member
Rebecca	Education programs coordinator
Reta	Former development director during 2011
Roy	Local artist and retired art professor
Stacy	Development director during 2019
Ted	Collections manager
Zach	Local artist

Index

Note: Page numbers in *italics* denote figures.

Academy of Motion Picture Arts and Sciences standards 101
access/accessibility 54, 56, 57, 64, 69–75, 82–83, 100–101; disabled 41–42, 45
active listening 98, 105
adaptability xiii, 20
Adler, P. 8, 10
Adler, P. A. 8, 10
admission charges 69, 70, 81, 91
African Americans *see* black community
age of visitors 80, 81, 83
American Alliance of Museums (AAM) 3, 33, 83, 100, 101, 103
American Association of Museums *see* American Alliance of Museums
Americans for the Arts 35
Americans with Disabilities (ADA) requirements 41–42
artists of color 70, 71, 81–82
arts education xiii, 36–37, 45, 74, 82
Asian community 43
Association of Art Museum Directors (AAMD) 5, 100, 101, 103
Association of Fundraising Professionals (AFC) 52
Atkinson, P. 7

Bateson, G. 21
biological systems 22
black community 43, 71, 72, 81, 83
blockbuster shows 73
board of directors 49, 50–53, 63–64, 66; demographics xiv, 43–44, 50–51; diversity 44, 51, 64, 79, 84, 100, 101; expertise 51–52; qualifications 52–53, 64; roles and responsibilities 51; term of service 51, 64; women on 44

BoardSource 51
Bourdieu, P. 42, 74
Bravo Greater Des Moines 102–103
Buddhism xi, 1, 21–22, 105
building design xiv, 39–42, 45
Bunch, L. G. 101
bureaucracy 17

change: incremental model of 88, 104; in mental models and throughputs xiv, 25–28, 84–85, 88, 90, 91, 97, 98–99, 103, 104; policy xv, 99, 101; radical model of 2, 104–105; transformational 23–25, 47
chief executive officer (CEO) 49, 50, 53–55, 91; as communication liaison 59–60
chief financial officer (CFO) 50, 55, 61
civil rights movement 18
clustering 20
collaboration xv, 98, 105; among arts and cultural organizations xiii, 37–38, 45; among/within departments xiv, 58, 59, 61–63, 65, 67, 94
collections, diversity in 70
Collections Department *see* Curatorial Department
communications xv, 58–61, 63, 65, 67, 94, 98; inclusive 98
community demographics xiv, 43, *80*
community inputs xv, 22, 49, 103; lack of 46–47, 83, 92–93; and mental models 93, 96–97; *see also* evaluation of programs and exhibitions; funding; non-visitor surveys; visitor(s)
community—museum relationship *see* museum—community relationship

compartmentalized museum structure 17, 58, 61
COVID-19 pandemic 18
CreateNYC 102
cultural capital: building 74; lack of xiv, 42–43, 45
culture 71–72; organizational *see* workplace culture
Curatorial Department 56–57, 62, 65, 93–94; lack of communication 63
curators 27, 57, 62, 64

data analysis and interpretation 11–12
data collection 9–11; duration of 13; interviews 9–10; observations 10; visitor and non-visitor surveys 10–11; visual methods 11
Davis, G. F. 18, 20–23
Day of the Dead celebration 71–72
deaccessioning 101
DEAI (diversity, equity, access, and inclusion) 100–101
Death to Museums movement 18–19
debt, elimination of 76–77, 82, 90–92
decision-making, transparency in 59–61, 65, 67
deep ecology 21, 105
deep learning museum xv, 104–106
delegative leadership 55, 59
demographics 3, 93; board xiv, 43–44, 50–51; community xiv, 43, *80*; staff xiv, 44, 56; visitor xiv, 44, 45, 69, 80–84, 94
departments 49, *50*, 55–58; collaboration among xiv, 58, 59, 61–63, 65, 67, 94; non-networked structure 64–66, 93–94
Detroit Institute of Arts 102
Development/Marketing Department 57–58, 62–64
disabled access 41–42, 45
dismissal decisions 60–61, 99
diversity 2–3, 19, 70, 100–101; board 44, 51, 64, 79, 84, 100, 101; in exhibitions and programs 70–72, 81–82, 92, 94, 99–100; funding linked to 102, 103; of funding sources 92; leadership 44, 45; staff 44, 45, 64, 79, 84–85, 100, 101, 103, 104; visitor 44, 45, 82–83, 104
donors 23, 33, 35, 36, 39, 52, 54, 60, 70, 75–78, 90–93, 100–104
duration of study 13
dynamic equilibrium xv, 24, 86, 99

economic revitalization xiii, 33–35, 45
education 19, 22, 45; arts xiii, 36–37, 45, 74, 82
Education Department 56, 59, 62–65, 75, 94
educational levels 83; community 43; staff 44, 56; visitor 44, 45, 80, 81
elitism, perception of 27, 38–39, 42, 45–47, 104
emotional intelligence 25
endowments 76, 82, 90–92
environment: influence on organizations 18, 19–21; professional, stimulation of xv, 100–103
equilibrium: dynamic xv, 24, 86, 99; stale 24
equity 100–101
ethnicity *see* race and ethnicity
ethnography, longitudinal 4, 7–8
evaluation of programs and exhibitions 93, 95, 96, 103
evening events 69, 74
Everson Museum of Art, Syracuse, NY 101
exhibitions *see* programs and exhibitions
expertise, board 51–52

fear of art xiv, 42–43
feedback functions 21–24, 105; mutual effects of negative and positive 88–95; open systems organization xiv, *24, 89;* *see also* negative feedback function; positive feedback function
flexibility xiii, 20
Flood, R, L, 21
free admissions and services 70, 91, 92
funding xiii, 22, 35–36, 39, 45, 46, 89–92, 103–104; city funding 77–79, 90–92; diverse sources of 92; and elimination of debt 76–77, 82, 90–92; endowments 76, 82, 90–92; fees for programs and admissions 69, 70, 81, 91; linked to diversity 102, 103; mental models 90–91; networked and sustainable xv, 75–79, 82, 92, 102–104

gallery host program 75, 82, 84
Gazley, B. 52
gender issues: gender of visitors 80; *see also* women
generalizability 13, 14
Glesne, C. 9
Goleman, D. 25

governance 2, 3
Guston, P., retrospective exhibition 27

Hämäläinen, R. 25, 26, 66–67, 97, 98
Hamilton, H. 26, 98, 99
Hammersley, M. 7
Harlem on My Mind (MET exhibition) 83
Hatch, M. J. 6
hierarchical museum structure 17, 49
hierarchy, networked 20–21
hiring processes 60–61, 84, 85, 88, 99, 103
Hispanic community 43, 71–72, 81
holarchy xiii, 20
holistic approach 3, 7–8
household income 43, 81
human resources (HR) role 61
human—nature dichotomy 21
humanistic organizational theories 17–18

inclusion 2–3, 19, 83, 84, 86, 98–101
income, household 43, 81
inputs 49, 86, 88; *see also* community inputs
Institute of Museum and Library Services 102
intentional practice 97, 98
interdependence xiii, 1, 17, 19–23, 25, 67, 89, 98, 105
interpretivist epistemology 6–7, 10
interviews 9–10

Janes, R. R. 3, 17, 52, 84, 104
Jewish history 27, 71
Jung, Y. 9, 18, 19, 24, 25, 37, 45, 75, 83, 89, 90, 105

Kania, J. 24–26, 98, 99
Karp, I. 47
Korn, R. 97, 98
Kramer, M. 24, 25, 98

Laszlo, E. 25, 66
Latino community 43, 81
Lavine, S. D. 47
leadership 25–26, 44, 45, 53–55, 64, 99; change in 66; delegative 55, 59; down-to-earth 54–55; system xiv, 67, 91, 94
learning environment 85–86
learning organization 25–26, 99, 105; *see also* deep learning museum

listening, active 98, 105
local art 72–73
longitudinal ethnography 4, 7–8
Love, A. R. 19, 105
Low, T. L. 17

MacLeod, J. 7–8
Macy, J. 21–24, 26, 105
marital status of visitors 80
marketing 57–58, 64, 66, 94–95; *see also* Development/Marketing Department
Marzio, P. C. 99–100
Maxwell, J. A. 12
mechanical museum structure 17
mechanistic systems 20
member surveys 92–93
mental models xiii, xiv, 22–25, 47, 67, 86, 88, 104, 105; challenging/changing xiv, 25–28, 84–85, 88, 90–91, 97, 99, 103, 104; and community inputs 93, 96–97; funding 90–91; of throughputs (culture and structure) 25, 65–66, 93–94
methods and methodology 6–14; data analysis and interpretation 11–12; data collection 9–11; limitations of 13–14; longitudinal ethnography 4, 7–8; research design 8–9; symbolic perspective of 6–7, 10
Metropolitan Museum of Art 5, 83
mind—body dichotomy 21
modernist organization theories 17, 20
morphogenesis 23
morphostasis 22, 23
museum—community relationship, disconnected realities 38–47; building design xiv, 39–42, 45; demographics of community, board and staff, and visitors xiv, 43–44; elitist perception xiv, 38–39, 45–47; fear of art xiv, 42–43; lack of cultural capital xiv, 42–45; public funding of private museum 39, 46
museum—community relationship, interconnected realities 32–38, 45; collaboration among arts and cultural organizations 37–38, 45; economic revitalization xiii, 33–35, 45; filling arts education gap xiii, 36–37, 45; public and private partnership of funding xiii, 35–36, 45
Museum of Fine Arts, Boston 27
Museum of Fine Arts, Houston 27
museum structure xiv, 25, 28, 47, 49–58, 67, 88, 93, 99, 103, 104;

compartmentalized 17, 58, 61; disorganization and reorganization of 98–99; hierarchical 17, 49; mechanical 17
mutual belonging 21
mutual causality xi, xii, 1, 3, 21–24, 26, 49, 105

Naess, A. 21, 105
National Endowment for the Arts 102
National Gallery of Art, Washington, DC 27
natural ecosystem 20, 21
negative feedback function xii, xiii, xv, 22–25, 88, 92–95
networked funding model xv, 75–79, 82, 92, 102–104
networked hierarchy 20–21
new intelligibility 25, 26, 85–86, 88, 92
New York City (NYC) 102
non-visitor surveys 10–11, 80, 95–97, 103
nonprofit status 19, 35, 45, 46, 52, 100

observations 10
occupational background of visitors 81
O'Neill, M. 96
open systems organization, feedback functions xiv, *24, 89*
open systems theory xi, xii, xiii, 1–3, 18–26, 105
organic organizational models 17
organic systems 20
organization theories: humanistic 17–18; modernist 17, 20; in museums 17–18
organizational anthropology 4
organizational culture *see* workplace culture
organizational structure *see* museum structure
organizations, influence of environment on 18–21
otherness 7
outcomes, and outputs 69
outputs xiv, 3, 49, 69, 92; and outcomes 69; *see also* marketing; programs and exhibitions
outreach programs 69, 74, 82, 83

paradigm shift 2, 26–28, 105–106
participants *see* research participants
paticca samuppada 21
photography, as means of data collection 12
policy change xv, 99, 101

popular culture 73
positive feedback function xii, xiii, xiv–xv, 23–25, 27, 28, 67, 86, 88–92; external pressure points of xv, 89, 100–103; leverage points of xv, 89, 95–100, 103; transformation to sustainable funding model 89–92
poverty 43
professional environment, stimulation of xv, 100–103
programs and exhibitions xiv, 69–75, 84, 88, 93–94, 103; diversity in 70–72, 81–82, 92, 94, 99–100; evaluation of 93, 95, 96, 103; inclusiveness approach to 99–100; relatable 72–74
public goods, arts as 37
public school arts education 36–37, 45, 74, 82
public—private partnership xiii, 35–36, 45

qualitative method 7
questions, asking 98, 105

race and ethnicity 3, 43, 80, 81; board of directors 50–51; community 43, 71; staff 27, 44, 45, 56; visitors 45, 80, 81, 83; *see also* artists of color
racism 24, 27, 71, 104
rapport 9–10
reductionism 20–21
reflection, as leverage point for positive feedback function 96–97, 103
research design 8–9
research methodology *see* methods and methodology
research participants: developing rapport with 9–10; number and composition 13–14; openness of 13
research questions 2

Saarinen, E. 25, 26, 66–67, 97, 98
Sandell, R. 3, 17, 52, 84, 104
schools *see* public school arts education
scientific management 17
Scott, W. R. 18, 20–23
security guards 75
self, in Buddhist teachings 21
self-organization 23
self-stabilization 22–23
Senge, P. 24–26, 98, 99, 105
significance of the research 2–4
Silverman, L. H. 96
small-to medium-sized museums 5, 7

social activities 74
social anthropology 4
social justice issues 71
social media 58, 64, 95
social systems 20–22
socioeconomic status 3, 43, 45, 56, 83; *see also* demographics
soft management 17
Spradley, J. P. 9
staff: demographics xiv, 44, 56; diversity 44, 45, 64, 79, 84–85, 100, 101, 103, 104; educational levels 44, 56; female 56; hiring and dismissal processes 60–61, 84, 85, 88, 99, 103; race/ethnicity 27, 44, 45, 56; turnover 55–58, 64
stale equilibrium 24
standards, professional 100–101
status quo: challenging/changing 26, 66, 86, 88; maintenance of xiv, 21–25, 85–86, 88, 92–95, 104
structure *see* museum structure
subcultures 58, 59
subjectivity 13, 14
subsystems 20, 22
surveys: member 92–93; visitor and non-visitor 10–11, 80–81, 94–97, 103
symbolic perspective 6–7, 10
system leadership xiv, 67, 91, 94
systems intelligence xiii, xiv, 25–27, 66–67, 86, 88, 91, 97–99, 103, 105
systems thinking 25, 98
Systems Thinking in Museums (Jung and Love) 19

Tate Modern, London 27
tax exemptions 19, 35, 45, 46, 100
Taylor, F. W. 17
threshold fear 41, 42
throughputs of the museum: change in xiv, 25, 84–85, 88, 91, 97–98; culture xiv, 25, 47, 58–63, 88, 94, 98–99, 103, 104; disorganization and reorganization of 98–99; mental models 25, 65–66, 93–94; structure xiv, 25, 47, 49–58, 88, 93–94, 98–99, 103, 104
Törmänen, J. 25, 26, 66–67, 97, 98
transformational change 23–25, 47
transparency in decision-making 59–61, 65, 67

visitor(s): age of 80, 81, 83; demographics xiv, 44, 45, 69, 80–84, 94; diversity 44, 45, 82–83, 104; educational levels 44, 45, 80, 81; gender of 80; numbers 69, 70, 79–80, 82, 83, 94; occupational background 81; race/ethnicity 45, 80, 81, 83; surveys 10–11, 80–81, 94–97, 103
Viso, O. 57
visual methods of data collection 11
Von Bertanlanffy, L. 19–20, 22, 24, 99

Weber, M. 17
women: artists 70, 81–82; directors 44; staff 56
workplace culture xiv, 25, 28, 47, 58–63, 65, 67, 88, 94, 98–99, 103, 104

For Product Safety Concerns and Information please contact our EU
representative GPSR@taylorandfrancis.com
Taylor & Francis Verlag GmbH, Kaufingerstraße 24, 80331 München, Germany

www.ingramcontent.com/pod-product-compliance
Lightning Source LLC
Chambersburg PA
CBHW070310230426
43664CB00015B/2706